GW00585322

R7-50
D6

THE ILLUMINATED NAPLES BIBLE

(Old Testament)

14th-Century Manuscript

Introduction and Notes by

Eva Irblich

Text by

Gabriel Bise

Translations by G. Ivins and D. MacRae

Stuttafords
BOOK SHOP
CAPE TOWN

Crescent Books

Distributed by Crown Publishers, Inc.

Vienna, Austrian National Library, Ms. 1191.
Photos: Austrian National Library.

The publishers are sincerely grateful to Pr.-Dr. Otto Mazal, Keeper of the Department of Manuscripts at the National Library of Austria, and to his assistant, Dr. Eva Irblich, for their kind and valuable cooperation.

INTRODUCTION

Form and Content of the Manuscript.

The Department of Manuscripts of the Austrian National Library preserves, catalogued as Codex 1191, a manuscript which contains in one volume the text of the Old and New Testaments (fol. 1r-478v), together with an alphabetical index of Hebrew names in Latin (fol. 481r-522r). The book itself measures about 36 × 25.3 cm (14 1/2 × 10 inches) and comprises 522 parchment leaves. The text is laid out in two columns, each of 52 ink-ruled lines on sheets of well-prepared goatskin parchment such as was generally used in the Mediterranean area in the High and Late Middle Ages. The entire text of the Bible was copied some time after the middle of the 14th century by a single scribe in calligraphic Gothic book-script of an Italian type and medium size, the « Rotunda » script, used in Italy in the High Middle Ages for certain types of manuscripts. On folio 455v, at the end of the Apocalypse, he gives his name, Johannes, and might possibly be identical with the Joannes of Ravenna or Jannutius de Matrice who copied two other Bibles which the same studio in Naples illustrated and decorated just as sumptously as the Bible of the Austrian National Library, from which selected parts are reproduced here in color. These are the "Hamilton Bible" (Berlin, Kupferstichkabinett, MS. 78 E 3) and the Leuven Bible (Leuven, Katholiche Universiteit, Bibliotheek van de Faculteit der Godgeleeerdheid, formely Malines, Bibliothèque du Séminaire, MS. 1). The numbering of the biblical books is given in Roman numerals, the individual figures of the numerals being colored alternately red and blue. The Lombardic majuscules of the column titles, placed above the level of the text to make it easier to find a particular book, are painted alternately in the same way. In so doing the scribe, who must have come from Northern Italy, was following the French manner of Bible manuscript design.

The alphabetical index of Hebrew names, however, is by

a different, unidentified hand. It is written in Gothic book script (litteral textualis), the initial letters of the lexical entries being in Lombardic majuscules colored alternately blue and red.

The manuscript contains all the books of the Old and New Testaments in the Vulgate version drawn up by St. Jerome (died 420) and subsequently considered the approved text of the Scriptures. That is why the Letter to Paulinus and Preface to Desiderius, both by St. Jerome, are placed at the beginning of the manuscript. In Codex 1191 the sequence of the individual books of the Bible follows that of the Vulgate version; the sole exceptions are the Acts of the Apostles (New Testament), which come after, not before the Epistles of Paul, and the Psalms (Old Testament), which follow St. John's Apocalypse, are placed at the end of the Bible on pages 457r-478v. Here it is to be noted that the Psalms were written on a separate section of parchment leaves which at some time before the rebinding of the manuscript at a later date might well have been placed elsewhere in the codex—in the Old Testament. This is all the more likely in view of the fact that the page between St. John's Apocalypse and the Psalms (fol. 456), the last leaf of a section, is blank, a circumstance which indicates that the Bible originally ended here.

Genesis, Decoration and History of the Manuscript.

The codex is very richly and sumptuously illustrated and decorated. The production of such a large volume involved the work of several people, the exact number depending on the particular grade of sumptuousness intended. The most important task was the layout of the book, that is, the calculation of the space needed for the text and for the blank spaces in which the initial letters and miniatures would later be painted.

Copies of the Bible have been produced in every period of history since late Graeco-Roman times, each period producing its own types of book. From classical times only fragments or individual books of the Bible such as Genesis or the Gospels in Greek and Roman characters have come down to us. The size of the majuscules and the cost of parchment—used by scribes since the 4th century—can be seen as reasons why the lengthy text of the Scriptures was not written down in one-volume compendia. Despite this, so-called "pandects", containing the whole Scriptures in a single volume, have been indentified in Spain in the first half of the 7th century. Besides the customary copying of individual books of the Bible in separate codices, the reform of Latin script under Charlemagne in the second half of the 8th century introduced the Carolingian minuscule, which made it possible to copy lengthy texts in a more compact manner. The Carolingian minuscule with its upper and lower strokes, fitted neatly into a four-line system. As a consequence of this new development the Bible, Christendom's most revered book, was copied on a larger scale than before in the great monastic centers of Europe. The abbey of Tours on the Loire played a leading role in this process in the 8th and early 9th centuries under Alcuin (died 804), producing in its scriptorium magnificent pandects containing the complete Bible text. The inner book of such a volume measures about 51 × 38 cm (20 1/2 × 15 inches) and contains 420-450 leaves, for which the skins of 210-225 animals (in Western Europe, sheep) were required. The skin of a fully-grown animal, once its extremities had been trimmed off, produced only a double leaf or bifolium (51 × 76 cm, 20 1/2 × 30 1/2 inches). As winter stall-feeding was as yet unknown to mediaeval agriculture, sheep and goats could only reach their full size in those areas of Europe with favourable climatic conditions where they could graze in winter in the open. This was the case in England, the Loire region and the Mediterranean area. If we consider that the manuscript described here measured 36 × 25.5 cm (14 1/2 × 10 inches), we can assume that the skin of a fully-grown goat produced two double leaves and that the manuscript required approximately 130 skins.

In Italy the so-called "giant Bible" (roughly 75 × 50 cm or 30 × 20 inches) appeared in the 11 th century, at the same time as the Investiture Struggle. From the Gothic period onwards the most diverse formats were used, script and artistic presentation being in proportion to the size of the

No. IIII.
N. 4
Theol. L. MS

Incipit epistola sancti Ieronimi presbiteri ad paulinum presbiterum de omnibus divine historie libris.

Frater Ambrosius tua michi munuscula perferens detulit et suavissimas litteras que a principio amicitiarum fidem probate iam fidei et veteris amicitie preferebant. Vera enim illa necessitudo est et Christi glutino copulata, quam non utilitas rei familiaris, non presentia tantum corporum, non subdola et palpans adulatio, sed dei timor et divinarum scripturarum studia conciliant. Legimus in veteribus historiis quosdam lustrasse provincias, novos adisse populos, maria transisse, ut eos quos ex libris noverant coram quoque viderent. Sicut Pitagoras memphiticos vates. Sic Plato Egyptum et Architam Tarentinum eamdemque oram Ytalie que quondam magna Grecia dicebatur laboriosissime peragravit, ut qui Athenis magister erat et potens, cuiusque doctrinas achademie gymnasia personabant, fieret peregrinus atque discipulus, malens aliena verecunde discere quam sua impudenter ingerere. Denique cum litteras quasi toto fugientes orbe persequitur, captus a piratis et venundatus etiam tyranno crudelissimo paruit, captivus, vinctus et servus. Tamen quia philosophus maior emente se fuit. Ad Titum Livium lacteo eloquentie fonte manantem de ultimis Hispanie Galliarumque finibus quosdam venisse nobiles legimus, et quos ad contemplationem sui Roma non traxerat, unius hominis fama perduxit. Habuit illa etas inauditum omnibus seculis celebrandumque miraculum, ut urbem tantam ingressi aliud extra urbem quererent. Apollonius sive ille magus ut vulgus loquitur, sive philosophus ut Pitagorici tradunt, intravit Persas, pertransivit Caucasum, Albanos, Scythas, Massagetas, opulentissima Indie regna penetravit, et ad extremum latissimo Phison amne transmisso pervenit ad Bragmanas, ut Hyarcam in throno sedentem aureo et de Tantali fonte potantem inter paucos discipulos de natura, de moribus ac de cursu siderum audiret docentem. Inde per Elamitas, Babilonios, Chaldeos, Medos, Assyrios, Parthos, Syros, Phenices, Arabes, Palestinos, reversus Alexandriam, perrexit ad Ethiopiam, ut gymnosophistas et famosissimam solis mensam videret in sabulo. Invenit ille vir ubique quod disceret, et semper proficiens semper se melior fieret. Scripsit super hoc plenissime octo voluminibus Philostratus. Quid loquar de seculi hominibus, cum apostolus Paulus vas electionis et magister gentium, qui de conscientia tanti in se hospitis loquebatur: An experimentum queritis eius qui in me loquitur Christus? post Damascum Arabiamque lustratam ascenderit Ierosolimam ut videret Petrum, et mansit apud eum diebus quindecim. Hoc enim misterio ebdomadis et ogdoadis futurus gentium predicator instruendus erat. Rursumque post annos quatuordecim assumpto Barnaba et Tito exposuit apostolis evangelium, ne forte in vacuum curreret aut cucurrisset. Habet nescio quid latentis energie viva vox actus, et in aures discipuli de auctoris ore transfusa fortius sonat. Unde et Eschines cum Rodi exularet, et legeretur illa Demosthenis oratio quam adversus eum habuerat, mirantibus cunctis atque laudantibus suspirans ait: Quid si ipsam audissetis bestiam sua verba resonantem? Nec hoc dico quod sit aliquid in me tale quod vel possis vel velis discere, sed quod ardor tuus et discendi studium etiam absque nobis per se probari debeat. Ingenium docile et sine doctore laudabile est. Non quid invenias, sed quid queras consideramus. Mollis cera et ad formandum facilis, etsi artificis et plastis cessent manus, tamen virtute totum est quicquid esse potest. Paulus apostolus ad pedes Gamalielis legem Moysi et prophetas didicisse se gloriatur, ut armatus spiritualibus telis postea doceret confidenter. Arma enim militie nostre non carnalia sunt, sed potentia deo ad destructionem munitionum, cogitationes destruentes, et omnem altitudinem extollentem se adversus scientiam dei, et captivantes omnem intellectum ad obediendum Christo, et parati subiugare cunctam

LIII

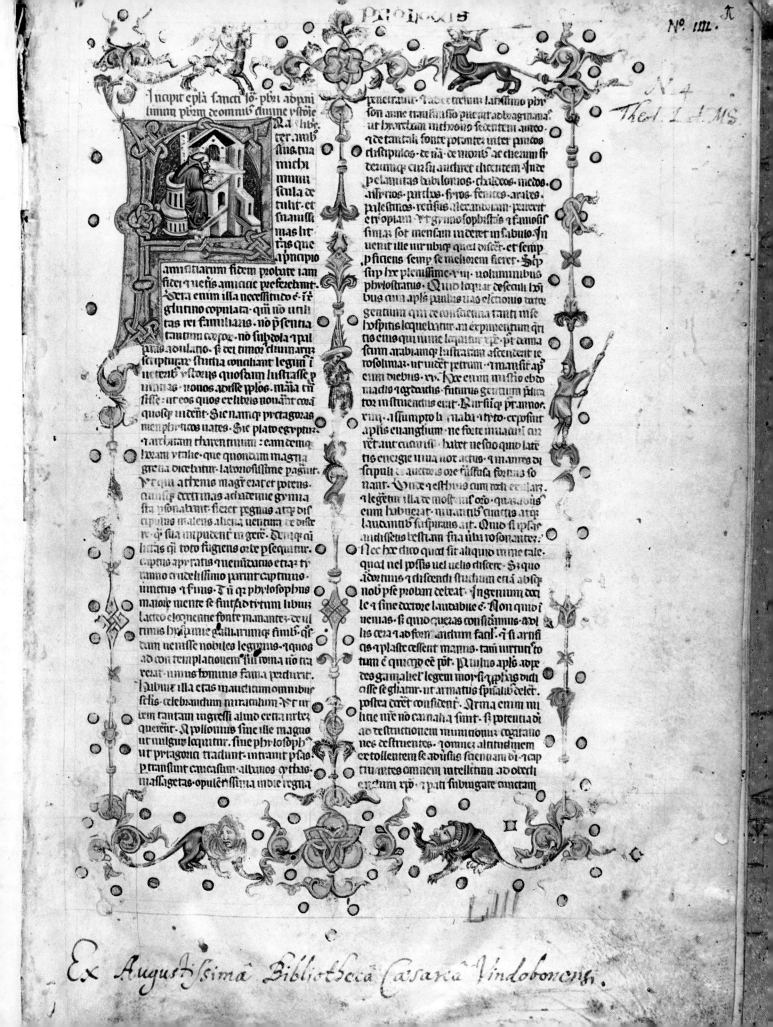

Ex Augustissima Bibliotheca Caesarea Vindobonensi.

book. De luxe editions made for courtly patrons were always large in size, while manuscripts for everyday use by theologians were produced in a more convenient format.

Once the Roman numerals for the chapters of the various books and the titles of the books as column titles had been put in, the work of the scribe Johannes and the rubricator was finished. The unbound sheets were then hended over to the studio, where a highly-organised team painted in the small initials, decorated initials and miniatures. This studio was situated in Naples and illuminated manuscripts for the court of Anjou and the surrounding area.

Each chapter begins with a small two— to four-line initial letter on a ground of gold leaf with a branching tracery of leaves colored pink, blue and green. The letters themselves, filled with decorative geometric and foliage patterns, stand out vividly, as the colors are finely nuanced by an admixture of opaque white. The branching traceries are accompanied by gold dots outlined in black, a feature which is typical of Italian illuminating. Fine dots in the gold leaf of the background of the initials increase the vivid effect and give the impression of embossed gold. In total the Bible contains 1398 such initials, in which the work of two hands can be seen. Of the four artists who had a share in the artwork, Miniaturist I painted the initial letters on the pages 3r-280v and Miniaturist II those in pages 281v-478v.

As well as the initial letters, with their lively forms and glowing gold and colors, 166 pages are provided with magnificent borders which enclose the text on all four sides. There is also an additional vertical border separating one column from another. These borders are made up of colored stems with lobed leaves, interlaced knots and geometrical decorations painted in blue, pink, green and gold and embellished with gold dots and droplet shapes outlined in black, and figures, angels, clerics and animals, the latter being fabulous beasts rendered in a naturalistic manner. In the artwork of the borders, too, the individual work of the four miniaturists can be distinguished. Thus Miniaturist I, who executed the borders on pages 1r-20v and four other branching traceries, shows in his treatment of the grotesque ornamentation and battle scenes the influence of the French school of illumination, which in the late 13th and also in the 14th century exhibited a preference for grotesque figures both human and animal.

Miniaturist II, influenced by the Sienna school, produced the borders and branching traceries on pages 21r, 21v and 457r-478v, which in their similar use of grotesque ornamentation are clearly related to those of Miniaturist I, but are dinstinguished from them by their use of color (orange and green being predominant) and by the pointed and spiny leaves of their branching traceries.

Only the borders of pages 23v and 24r can be ascribed to Miniaturist III, probably an assistant of Miniaturist I. The individual decorations are larger and less varied, whilst the grotesque ornamentations with their black interior drawing are more carefully shaped.

The borders done by Miniaturist IV, the main illuminator of this Bible and obviously Florentine in technique, are to be found on pages 25r-450v and are quite different from the others. They are simpler in design and consist of blue, red and green rods embellished with knots, curling leaves, flowers or geometrical ornament. The corners and junctions of the individual borders are given additional emphasis by large rhombi, interlaced ornaments or quatrefoils on a gold ground. Another characteristic of the borders done by Miniaturist IV is the consistent embellishment of the upper and lower borders with grotesque ornamentation in madder red, bright green and brown. These grotesqueries depict the hind quarters of a dog-like animal, with a caricatured animal head, sometimes wearing a cap and loosely wrapped in cloth.

In considering the illuminations of the manuscript one must take into account its 39 large initials, which include painted figures or small scenes. The initial depict, for example, St. Jerome as the author of various Bible prefaces, sitting at his desk, prophets as authors of the prophetic books of the Old Testament, St. Paul in 13 instances as author of his Epistles, St. James, St. Peter in 2 instances, St. John in 3 instances, Judas and finally St. John as author of the Apocalypse. These initial pictures were painted by Miniaturist I (fol. 1r-269v) and Miniaturist IV (fol. 410v-450v). The nine initial pictures for

the Psalms, including a picture of King David and other illustrations, are by Miniaturist II (fol. 457r-473v). The picture of St. Jerome in monastic habit at the beginning of the index of Hebrew names can be ascribed to Miniaturist IV on stylistic grounds.

The finest part of the artwork is the 184 miniatures which adorn the Bible, of which a selection of those from the Old Testament is reproduced here. The work of the four miniaturists is distributed in the following manner: the miniatures for Genesis on fol. 4r-19v are by Miniaturist I, those for Genesis on fol. 20v-21v and for the Psalms on fol. 457r-473v by Miniaturist II, those for the end of Genesis and the beginning of Exodus (fol. 23v and 24r) are by Miniaturist III and two for Genesis (fol. 22r and 23r) together with all the rest from Exodus to the Apocalypse (fol. 25r-455v) are by Miniaturist IV. The miniatures are set in approximately square panels edged in red, blue and green, for which blank spaces have been left in the columns. Only in Genesis and the Apocalypse are they place in the wide margin underneath the columns and extending the width of both columns.

Of the four artists concerned Miniaturist I is very significant. He drew his inspiration from French models, a fact which can be deduced from his treatment of backgrounds in the chequered French style and from the form and composition of individual figures, which derive their vividness from varied nuances of color. The scenes are drawn in a lively style and attain a genuine dramatic effect when they depart from their French models. In the miniatures for the story of the Creation the French influence is particularly plain, but the representation of God as the Trinity imitates French iconography, as can be seen equally clearly in the same miniatures in the "Hamilton Bible" (Berlin, Kupferstichkabinett, MS. 78 E 3). The foreground is made up of landscape elements, trees and mountains being treated in stylised, non-naturalistic manner. The background ends in a flat tapestry effect. The architecture indicates no skill in perspective. The artist's palette is rich, strong blues, yellows and orange predominating over light greens, reddish browns

Dixit dominus ad moysen. Ecce consti
tui te deum pharaonis. et aaron frater tuus
erit propheta tuus. tu loqueris ei omnia que man
do. ille loquetur ad pharaonem. ut dimittat fi
lios israel de terra sua. Sed ego indurabo cor ei
us et multiplicabo signa ostenta mea in terra
egypti. et non audiet vos. Immittamque
manum meam super egyptum. et educam ex
ercitum et populum meum filios israel de terra egypti
per iudicia maxima. et scient egyptii quod
ego sum dominus. qui extenderim ma
num meam super egyptum. et eduxerim fili
os israel de medio eorum. Fecit itaque moyses
et aaron sicut preceperat dominus ita egerunt.
Erat autem moyses .lxxx. annorum. et aa
ron .lxxxiii. quando locuti sunt ad pharaonem.
Dixitque dominus ad moysen et aaron. Cum
dixerit vobis pharao. ostendite signa. dices
ad aaron. Tolle virgam tuam et proice
eam coram pharaone. ac vertetur in colubrum.
Ingressi itaque moyses et aaron ad pharaonem.
fecerunt sicut preceperat dominus. Tulitque
aaron virgam coram pharaone et servis eius.
que versa est in colubrum. proiecitque eam in terram.
Vocavit autem pharao sapientes et maleficos.
et fecerunt et ipsi per incantationes egyptiacas.
et archana quedam similiter. proieceruntque singuli
virgas suas. que verse sunt in dracones. sed de
voravit virga aaron. virgas eorum. Indu
ratumque est cor pharaonis et non audivit eos.
sicut preceperat dominus. Dixit autem dominus
ad moysen. Induratum est cor pharaonis non
vult dimittere populum. Vade ad eum mane.
Ecce egredietur ad aquas. et stabis in occur
sum eius super ripam fluminis. et virgam
que versa est in draconem tolles in manu
tua. dicesque ad eum. Dominus deus hebreorum
misit me ad te dicens. Dimitte populum me
um. ut sacrificet michi in deserto. et usque ad
presens audire noluisti. Hec igitur dicit dominus.
In hoc scies quod dominus sim. Ecce percutiam
virga. que in manu mea est aquam fluminis
et vertetur in sanguinem. Pisces quoque qui sunt
in fluvio morientur. et putrescent aque. et
affligentur egyptii bibentes aquam flu
minis. Dixit quoque dominus ad moysen.
Dic aaron. Tolle virgam tuam et exten
de manum tuam super aquas egypti. et super flu
vios eorum et rivos ac paludes. et omnes
lacus aquarum. ut vertantur in sanguinem.
et sit cruor in omni terra egypti. tam in ligne
is vasis quam in saxeis. Feceruntque ita moy
ses et aaron. sicut preceperat dominus. Et ele
vans virgam percussit aquam fluminis coram
pharaone et servis eius. que versa est in sang
uinem. et pisces qui erant in flumine mor
tui sunt. Computruitque flumen. et non
poterant egyptii bibere aquam fluminis. et fu
it sanguis in tota terra egypti. Feceruntque
similiter malefici egyptiorum incantationibus
suis. Et induratum est cor pharaonis. nec
audivit eos. sicut preceperat dominus. Avertitque
se et ingressus est domum suam. nec apposuit
cor etiam hac vice. Foderunt autem omnes
egyptii per circuitum fluminis aquam
ut biberent. Non enim poterant bibere de aqua
fluminis. Impletique sunt septem dies
postquam percussit dominus flumen. VIII

Dixit dominus ad moysen. Ingre
dere ad pharaonem et dices. Hec dicit
dominus. dimitte populum meum ut sacrificet
michi. Sin autem nolueris dimittere.

and blue-greys.

The technique of Miniaturist II, on the other hand, derives from the Sienese tradition, as can be seen from the light green shadows in his faces and from his sharply-drawn figures. The artist's individuality appears clearly in his powerful, light colors and his combination of orange-yellows, sky-blues and gold.

Miniaturist III illuminated only two pages of the manuscript, in which the miniatures are of a coarser quality. Stylistically they incline towards those of Miniaturist I but do not attain his delicacy in the treatment of figures and combination of colors. The painter must have been an assistant of Miniaturist I.

Miniaturist IV, who carried out the majority of the illuminations, gives a quite different impression. In all his pictures his compositions lack variety but have a formal beauty. His figures appear singly or in groups against a background of gold or ultramarine, their heads forming a single line. Often several events are depicted on two levels of the same picture. The figures wear long, vividly-drawn draped robes, the soldiers pink, blue and occasionally metallic colored armor and helmets. The mountains are bare in the manner of stage scenery and stereotyped in the style of trecento landscape painting, whilst the animals, including cattle, horses and camels, are magnificent. Brilliant reds and blues predominate in his finely-nuanced palette, which resembles stylistically Tuscan trecento painting. He must have been trained in a Florentine studio before coming to Naples. The miniatures for the Apocalypse are also by his hand. Painted in bright colors, gold and harsh yellows, against a deep blue background, they demonstrate his amazing imaginative gifts in the illustration of the visionary text.

This Bible, produced in Naples' greatest studio in the thirteen-fifties, must have been completed about 1360. Its magnificent illuminations, particularly in the Old Testament, are the work of an artist working in the French tradition, a Sienese-Neapolitan and a Florentine painter. As an iconographic work of art it does not exist in isolation; its Old Testament artwork shows the influence of models inspired in Naples by the House of Anjou. The line of models stretches from the Apocalypse paintings in Santa Maria Donna Regina (after 1317) via the panel painting of the Apocalypse from the thirteen-thirties in the Staatsgalerie in Stuttgart, the cycle of Old Testament scenes in the church of Santa Maria Incoronata (circa 1340) and the Leuven Bible to the Hamilton Bible (circa 1350). The manuscripts of this group, which were produced between 1340 and 1360, drew on older Neapolitan paintings commissioned by the House of Anjou, and particularly by Robert of Anjou.

It is not known who commissioned this magnificent Bible, though the as yet unidentified coat of arms of a previous owner is to be found on pages 291v and 349v. The copiousness and richness of the illuminations do however indicate that the patron was close to the Court of Anjou. The manuscript itself gives no clues as to its subsequent fate. In the 16th century it was already in Habsburg hands. At the very latest by 1575 the manuscript was assigned to the Hofbibliothek in Vienne, as is shown by the fact that the back of its final leaf has a classification-mark in the handwriting of Hugo Blotius, the first Prefect of the Hofbibliothek from 1575 to 1608.

In 1752 when Gerard van Swieten (also Court Physician to the Empress Maria Theresia) was Prefect of the Hofbibliothek, the manuscript was given a plain parchment binding, the covers of which bore the imperial coat of arms in gold, the bookplate, as it were, of the Hofbibliothek.

Eva Irblich

... rex glie ...
rex glie. domini uirtutu3 ipe e re
AD te domine xxiiij. psal
leuaui aiam mea. deus me
ofido no erubescam. Neq3 irrid
inimici mei. et enim qui te expt
fundent. Confundantur ei omn
agentes sup uacue. Vias tuas d
monstra michi. et semitas tuas e
Dirige me in ueritate tua et doce m
es ds saluator meus et te sustinu
Reminiscere miserationu3 tuar dn
tuar que a sclo sunt. Delicta
tis mee. et ignorantias meas ne
ris. Scdm miaz tuam memento
pter bonitatez tuam domine.
rectus dns. ppt h dabit delinqu
uia. Diriget mansuetos in iud
bit mites uias suas. Vniuse u
et ueritas. requirentib testamtu
monia eius. Propter nom tuu d
abis pcto meo. multu e eni
homo qui timet dnm. legem st
i uia q elegit. Anima ei in bo
rabitur. et semen ei hreditabit
Firmamentu e dominus timen
et testamtum ipius ut manifes
Oculi mei semp ad dnm: qm
let de laqueo pedes meos. Resp
et miserere mei: qz unicus et paup
Tribulationes cordis mei mult
sunt. de necessitatib meis erue

... decorem domus et locum ha-
bitationis glie tue. Ne pdas cu impiis
deus aiam mea: et cum uiris sanguinum
uitam mea. In quorum manibus iniquita
tes sunt: dextera eorum repleta est munerib
bus. Ego autem in innocentia mea ingressus
sum: redime me et miserere mei. Pes meus
stetit in directo: in ecclesiis benedicam te
domine. xxvi. ps dd. pmus qñ liniretur.

Dominus il
luminatio
mea: et salus
mea quem time
bo. Dns pro
tector uite
mee: a quo
trepidabo.
Dum appropi
ant sup me
nocentes: ut edant carnes meas. Qui
tribulant me inimici mei: ipsi infirma
ti sunt et ceciderunt. Si consistant aduer
sum me castra: non timebit cor meum. Si
exurgat adu sum me plium: in hoc ego
sperabo. Unam peti a domino hanc re
quiram: ut inhabitem in domo dni omnib
diebus uite mee. Ut uideam uoluntatem
domini: et uisitem templum eius. Quoniam ab
scondit me in tabnaculo suo in die ma
lorum: ptexit me in abscondito tabnacli
sui. In petra exaltauit me: et nunc exaltauit
capud meum: sup inimicos meos. Cir

BIBLIOGRAPHY

P. d'Ancona, La Miniature italienne du xᵉ au xviᵉ siècle. Paris and Bruxelles 1925, 47-48.

H. J. Hermann, Die italienischen Handschriften des Dugento und Trecento 3. Neapolitanische und toskanische Handschriften der zweiten Hälfte des 14. Jahrhunderts. Leipzig 1930, 250-288. (Beschreibendes Verzeichnis der illuminierten Handschriften in Österreich, N.F. 5, 3). Here quotations from literature.

Les principaux manuscrits à peintures de la Bibliothèque Nationale de Vienne. Première partie : Manuscrits italiens. Paris 1937, 14-16. (Bulletin de la Société française de Reproductions de Manuscrits à peintures, 20).

A. Schmitt, Die Apokalypse des Robert von Anjou, in: Panthéon 28/6 (1970) 475-503.

B. Fischer, Die Alkuin-Bibeln, in: Die Bibel von Moutier-Grandval. British Museum Add. Ms. 10 546. Bern 1971, 49-98, besonders 64-65 und Anm. 182 auf 65.

In preparation:

Studies of 14th-century Neapolitan Bibles, by Hanns Swarzenski.

I. GENESIS

THE CREATION OF THE HEAVENLY BODIES AND THE ANIMALS.

Jehovah created the heavens and the earth. After separating them from the waters he formed the blue disk of the firmament, and, in its midst, he drew from the darkness the yellowish globe of our earth, which was bathed in light, and gave it life. In the person of the Trinity—God the Father, with his bushy beard, the lean-faced Son and the Holy Ghost, in the form of a dove, resting on his shoulder—the Creator, clad in a white cloak and holding a magician's wand, watched over the wonderful things which he, in his omnipotence, had made: the sun, which was the light of day, the moon which shed its much more modest radiance by night, the animals grazing in the fields and the fish beneath the restless waves.

THE CREATION OF EVE

Once the seven days of the Creation were over, Jehovah took some clay, fashioned it in his own likeness and breathed into the nostrils of his model the breath of life. Adam, the first man, was born; he lived contentedly in the Garden of Eden which had been planted for him. Since it was wrong for man to live alone Jehovah then created Eve, the first woman, out of a rib which he had taken from Adam's side as he lay sleeping under a tree. The couple which he had created in his own image were thenceforth to rule the world, drinking the water of the streams, eating the flesh of fish and animals and of all fruits except for that of the Tree of the Knowledge of Good and Evil, which stood in the midst of the Garden of Eden.

ORIGINAL SIN.

Face to face in the innocence of their nudity, Adam and Eve were leading contented lives in the world of Eden when, all of a sudden, the most cunning of all the animals, the tempting serpent, crossed their path. Playing on the vanity of woman, he promised Eve that she would live for ever if she were to taste the forbidden fruit. Despite the Creator's stern warnings, the couple, their curiosity aroused, went over to the fatal tree. Eve fell into the trap set for her by the serpent lurking in the undergrowth, and, to their great misfortune, bit into the apple which she had just picked. She then gave it to Adam to taste.

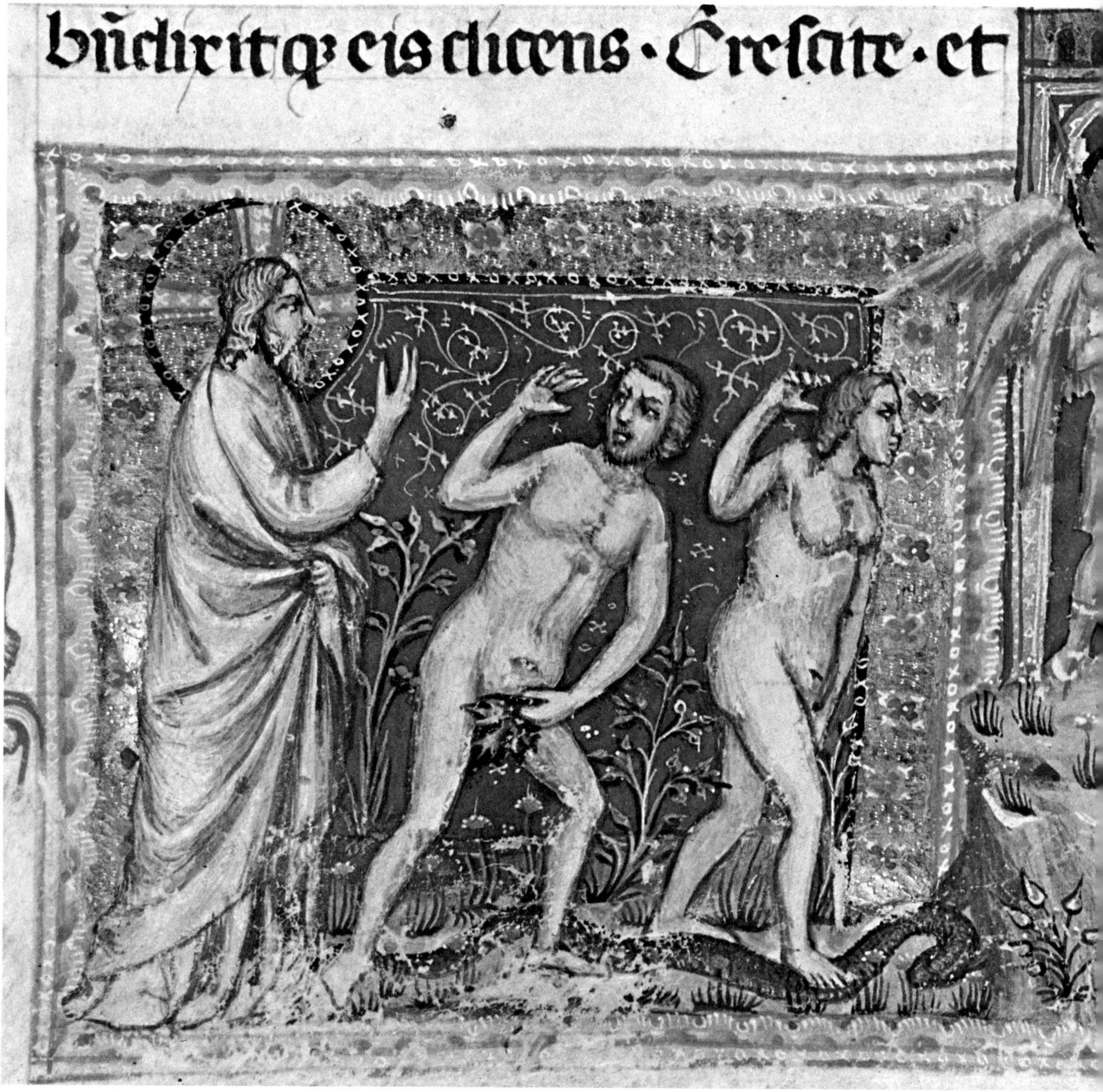

Adam and Eve are expelled from the Garden of Eden.

Aware of their guilt, Adam and Eve now became embarrassed by their nudity and hid their sexual organs under fig leaves. They took refuge among the foliage, listening fearfully for the approach of Jehovah, and trying vainly to escape his sovereign verdict. The evil serpent was

condemned to creep along the ground, while the two culprits were expelled from the Garden of Eden, whose gates were henceforth watched by the angel with the flashing sword. Clad in the animal skins which Jehovah had given them, they were sent forth to work the arid soil and lead lives of hardship and sweat before eventually dying and returning to the earth from which they had been taken.

THE FIRST VICTIM.

From the carnal union of Adam and Eve came forth Abel, the shepherd, and Cain, the plowman. Thanks to their work the flocks grew larger and the harvests were good, so that both of them made their offerings to Jehovah. Abel's offerings, purified by the flame of sacrifice, rose in a clear smoke towards the blue halo surrounding the benign hand of the Creator; but the sheaves of wheat lit by Cain sent their dark smoke downwards, to the ground. The tiller of the ground realized that Jehovah viewed his sacrifice with displeasure, and, suddenly overwhelmed by crazed hatred, he flung himself on his young brother and killed him.

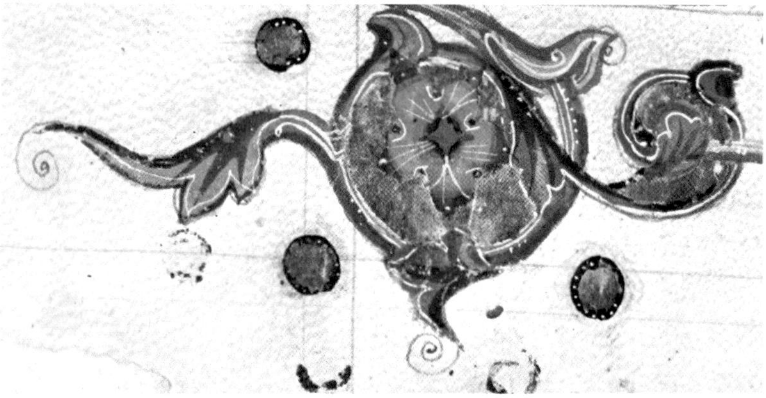

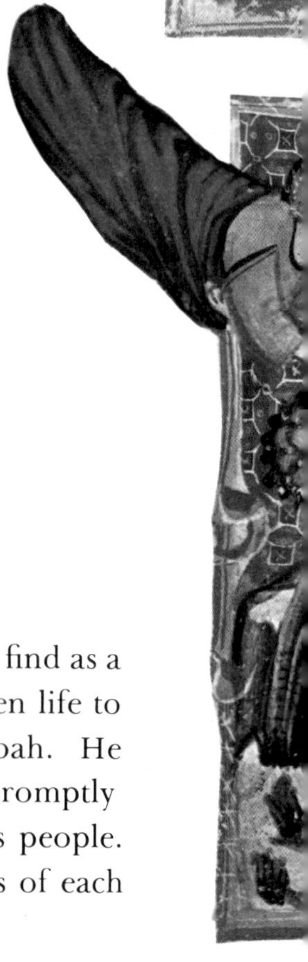

THE BUILDING OF THE ARK.

Mankind had became wicked: men thought nothing of seizing any women they could find as a means of quenching their carnal desires. Eventually Jehovah came to regret having given life to man and decided to wipe out the whole of Creation, with the exception of the wise Noah. He ordered him to build an ark of resinous woods and reeds soaked in pitch. Noah promptly complied, directing the work of the carpenters, who had been chosen from among his people. When the rains began to fall, he embarked in this ark with his family and two animals of each species.

THE FLOOD

For forty days the rain poured down ceaselessly upon the whole of Creation, engulfing the cities which had become corrupted by evil, the animals and the bounteous nature which had been made by the hands of Jehovah. The solitary Ark floated over the immensity of the resulting desolation; from a window in the side of the vessel, Noah watched for some sign that the cataclysm was over. Suddenly a dove flew in and settled on his shoulder; the olive branch which it carried in its beak showed clearly that the rains had stopped, the waters were about to recede and that nature was already beginning to recover.

NOAH'S SACRIFICE

The rains had stopped; the water had receded from the land and the ark had run aground on the slopes on Mount Ararat. Frisking about restlessly, the animals rushed out and started eagerly grazing on the first pastures which newly-found nature had provided for them. The survivors of mankind were the last to leave the ark. Noah's first concern was to build the altar of burnt offerings. Together with his three sons, Shem, Ham and Japheth, he offered his sacrifice to Jehovah on the altar, in order to seal the covenant uniting him to the Lord of creation.

THE BUILDING OF THE TOWER OF BABEL.

After the Flood Jehovah scattered mankind all over the face of the earth. Men originally spoke a single language and their arrogance eventually led them to disobey Jehovah by forming themselves into a group. Using stone and mortar they started building a city, and, in the middle of it, a tower of bricks and pitch reaching up into the sky, as a point around which they could rally. Sensing the vanity of their motives, Jehovah decided to confuse the language of the builders: thenceforth they uttered only an unintelligible muddle of sounds, and, overcome by discord, they finally abandoned their project and went their various ways.

THE DESTRUCTION OF SODOM.

Jehovah had granted his protection to Abraham and to his numerous descendants. However, the sexual perversion of the inhabitants of Sodom angered him; despite the pleadings of the old patriarch, he decided to destroy by fire that den of iniquity. His angels went to the city and spent the night in the house of Lot, its only just citizen. They urged him to leave his house before dawn, with his wife and his two daughters, and go up into the mountains. No sooner had the sun peeped over the horizon than a rain of sulfur transformed the city into an inferno, while Lot and his family, led by the angels, fled without looking back. Lot's wife, however, did yield to her curiosity and glanced back at the blazing city—whereupon she was turned into a pillar of salt.

THE SACRIFICE OF ISAAC.

Wishing to put the venerable patriarch to the test, Jehovah asked him to sacrifice his young son Isaac. Abraham did not hesitate one instant. Having chopped the wood for the burnt offering, he saddled his ass, and, followed by two young men, he set out with Isaac. When they reached the foot of the mountain chosen by Jehovah the party halted, and Abraham asked the young men to stay with the ass. After loading the firewood on his son's shoulders, the patriarch took the flame and knife, went up the mountain, bound his son on the sacrificial wood and was just about to immolate him when the arm of Jehovah stopped him. Just a short distance away was the animal which he was to offer in place of Isaac—a ram caught in a thicket by its horns.

JOSEPH COMPLAINS TO HIS AGEING FATHER JACOB ABOUT HIS BROTHERS.

Abraham died at a very old age. His offspring peopled the earth, spending their lives cultivating the soil and raising their flocks. Amongst his heirs the ageing Jacob, who was the father of eleven children, quite clearly favored the youngest son, Joseph. His fondness for him meant that the young man was a constant target for the heavy sarcasm of his ten elder brothers. There could be no brotherhood between these shepherds who, though of the same flock, had been born of the different wives of the patriarch. The young man with the "coat of many colors" eventually opened his heart to Jacob on this subject, telling him of his distress at the constant malice of his brothers.

THE BROTHERS BRING TO JACOB THE BLOODSTAINED COAT OF THE YOUNG JOSEPH

Joseph was touched by the affection of his ageing father, and the pride which swelled up in his heart caused him to have two dreams, in which his young person was deified in the eyes of his brothers. Their rancor soon turned to hatred; after plotting his death they decided to fling him to the bottom of a dry water tank,

having first taken from him his coat of many colors. Seizing a ram they slit its throat and soaked the coat in the blood. With feigned anxiety they returned to their father's house, handed the bloodstained coat to Jacob and told him that the youth, who had obviously set out to look for them, must have lost his way in the desert, and that they had found the remains of his body which had been devoured by a wild beast. The griefstricken old man tore his garments and, with Rebecca at his side, wept disconsolately over the loss of his favorite son.

JOSEPH IS SOLD TO THE ISHMAELITES

Before returning to their old father and handing him the bloodstained coat, the brothers had noticed that a caravan of rich Ishmaelite merchants, on their way to Egypt, were approaching the water tank. It then occurred to them to sell their young brother to them, thus avoiding the punishment which they would have incurred for the act of fratricide. Having brought the prisoner out of his dark place of confinement they clad him in a robe and introduced him to the strangers. The merchants, delighted with such an unexpected bargain, handed them twenty pieces of silver and, taking Joseph with them, went on their way towards the land of the Pharaohs.

JOSEPH AND THE WIFE OF POTIPHAR.

Thanks to the protection of Jehovah, the young Hebrew rose in the world and became his master's steward. Potiphar's wife had also been impressed by his merits. Haunted by the beauty of his features she went so far as to lure him into her bed; Joseph, realizing that he could not betray his master's trust, panicked and fled, leaving his coat in the hands of the seductress. Hearing her cries, the entire household ran to the scene and found her in evident distress, proclaiming her innocence and the brazen effrontery of the young Hebrew. The master then arrived himself and had the suspect flung in jail, in the company of the prisoners of the king.

JOSEPH INTERPRETS THE PHARAOH'S DREAM.

One night the Pharaoh had a dream in which he saw, rising from the Nile, seven fat cows followed by seven lean cows which devoured them; he also saw seven thick ears of corn come out of the ground, followed by seven lean ears which engulfed them. None of the court magicians could interpret this dual dream. On the proposal of the chief butler Joseph was taken from the jail, dressed in new clothes and brought before the king. No sooner had he told him of his dream than the Hebrew slave, inspired by Jehovah, told him that there would be seven years of abundance followed by seven years of shortages and urged him to store as much corn as possible in order to survive. The Pharaoh saw the wisdom of this reply, entrusted Joseph with the management of his palace and bestowed many honors upon him.

JOSEPH AND HIS BROTHERS.

Jacob had been told that Egypt was full of grain. He thus instructed his sons to go there and buy ample reserves for their land of Canaan. When they were ushered into the presence of the chief steward they bowed down before their brother without recognizing him; when he, having recognized them, called them spies, they protested their innocence. Egypt had no need for their silver purses; on Joseph's orders they were thrown into prison for three days. When they were released they were required to leave one of their number as a hostage, before they returned to Canaan with foodstuffs, but Joseph insisted that they should come back to Egypt with their young brother Benjamin who had been left at home during the first trip.

JOSEPH IS RECOGNIZED BY HIS BROTHERS.

Famine was rife in the land of Canaan. Jacob had decided to send his sons to Egypt together with Benjamin; they were to take gifts for the powerful lord from their own country, the silver purses rejected by the Egyptians on their first trip and more purses intended as payment for a new consignment of corn! When Joseph saw his young brother he gave orders for the visitors to be accomodated in his own house, their sacks to be filled with corn, and their silver purses to be put back inside those sacks. Moreover, he had his own silver goblet slipped into Benjamin's bag. In the morning the Hebrews left the city, but they had gone only a short way when they were stopped by an official who searched their bags and discovered the goblet. When they were brought before Joseph the sons of Jacob sought to explain away this mysterious theft. Seeing their plight, Joseph ordered his entire household to leave the premises, brought his brothers in and, behind closed doors, revealed his true identity to them. They fell on their knees and then rose to warmly embrace their long-lost brother.

Jacob blesses the two sons of Joseph, Ephraim and Manasseh.

Jacob lay on his bed, laid low by illness, his eyes dull with age. Seventeen years had now passed since he had left the land of Canaan with all of his kin to settle, by kind permission of the Pharaoh, on the rich soil of Egypt. He had known the great joy of finding once again his favorite son and of receiving from him the final consolation of learning that, after his death which he now felt was imminent, his body would be taken back to the land of his ancestors. One day Joseph went to the patriarch with the two sons who had been born to him in Egypt, Ephraim and Manasseh. To Joseph's immense surprise the old man placed his right hand on the head of the younger son, Ephraim, and his left hand on that of the older Manasseh, thus showing that the offspring of the younger son would be very numerous. Then, having adopted both of them as his own children, he blessed them saying: "May you be blessed in Israel!"

The death of Jacob.

Sensing that his end was near, Jacob gathered his twelve sons about him to bless them and announce to them the destiny of each of the tribes of Israel placed under their protection. With his last breath he reiterated the desire to be buried in the grave in the land of Canaan where Abraham and Isaac already lay. He then died. His passing was lamented throughout Egypt and even in the Pharaoh's court. Joseph had the royal doctors embalm the body and then buried it in Palestine.

Do t[ibi] partem unam ex[tra] fr[atr]es tuos. q[ua]m tuli
d[e] manu amorrei in gladio [et] arcu meo.

II

Vocavit aut[em] iacob
filios suos [et] ait. Congregamini ut an
nuntiem que ventura sunt vob[is] dieb[us] no
uissimis. Congregamini [et] audite filij
iacob. audite isr[ae]l patrem u[est]r[u]m. Ruben
p[ri]mogenit[us] m[eu]s. [et] tu fortitudo mea: [et] p[ri]n

II. EXODUS.

THE CHILDREN OF ISRAEL IN EGYPT.

After Jacob large numbers of Israelites had come to live in Egypt, under the protection of Joseph. Taking their livestock with them they had fled the famine which was ravaging their own country and reached the land of Egypt, in which corn grew in abundance. Being both hard-working and fertile they extended their power throughout the country and grew to such numbers that the Egyptians, after the deaths of Joseph and the good Pharaoh, became quite alarmed. The new king made the Hebrews do forced labor—in sharp contrast to their previous existence—in order to make life as unpleasant as possible for them; he even ordered the midwives to kill off new-born male Jewish babies.

MOSES AND THE BURNING BUSH.

As a child Moses, who was himself a miracle of the Nile, enjoyed the happy life of a Pharaoh's son. Yet he could see the endless harassment inflicted on his Hebrew compatriots, and his young heart rebelled. Hunted by the Pharaoh's police he fled to the land of Midian, where he found the happy pastoral life of his forefathers. While he was there Jehovah, faithful to his covenant with the patriarchs, sought him out and sent him back to help his people. He took him up Mount Horeb, in the middle of the desert, and addressed him from a perpetually burning bush. Jehovah was so deeply moved by the plight of the chosen people that he sent Moses to plead with the Pharaoh on behalf of the Hebrews and to prepare for their departure from the country.

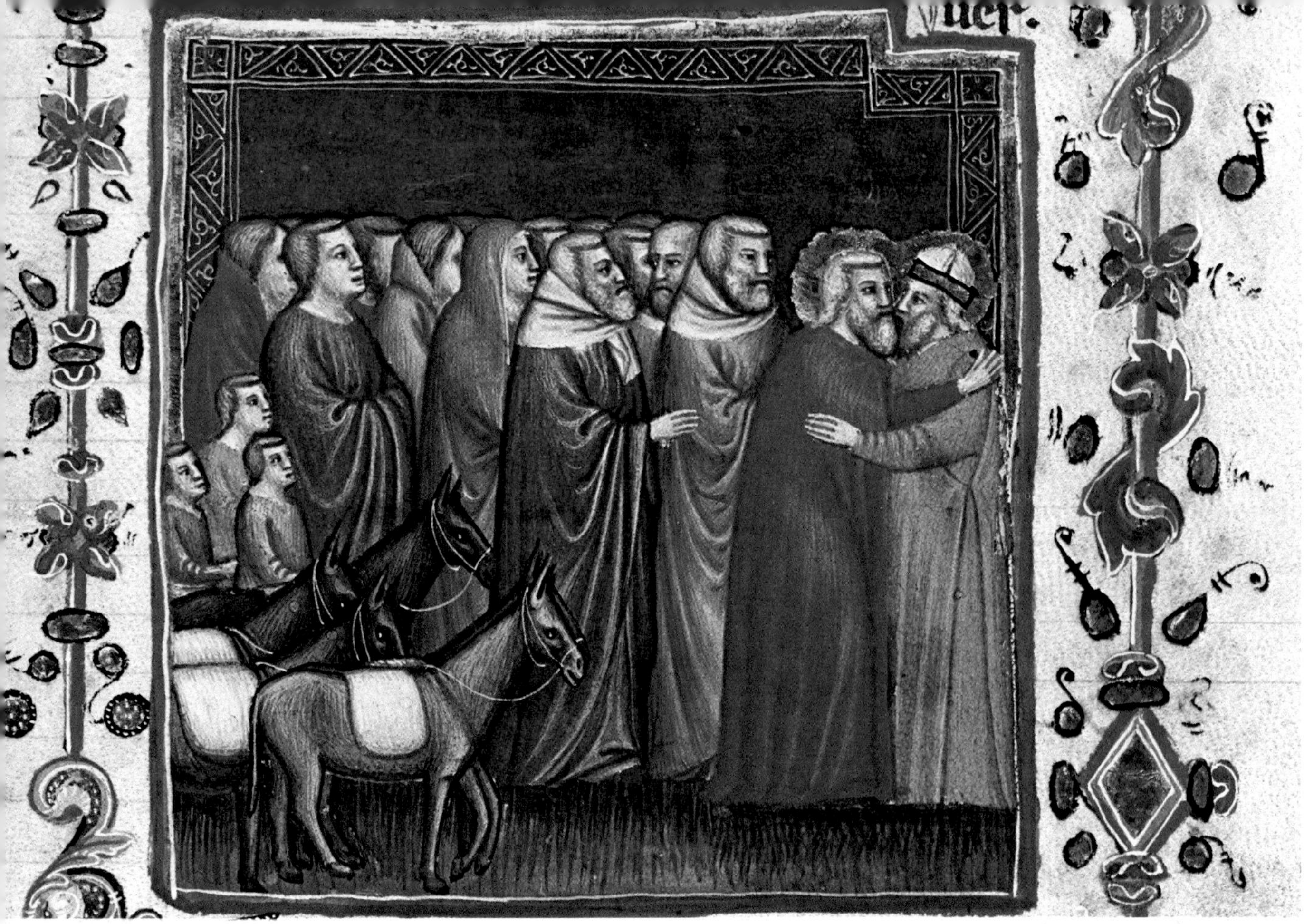

Moses and Aaron meet in the desert.

Moses was frightened when he thought of the dangers involved in such a grave mission and was extremely reluctant to accept it. How, he argued, could he, who was such a poor and unpersuasive speaker, win the support of the people and convince the king? Jehovah reminded Moses that his brother Aaron was renowned for his eloquence. He then handed him the rod which turned into a serpent, as a sign of his power. Guided by Jehovah, Moses and Aaron met in the desert and, despite the efforts of the Egyptian police, managed to assemble all the elders of the tribes of Israel. Aaron convinced them with the help of Jehovah, and the Israelites, now feeling more confident, kneeled before the two brothers to thank them for their great compassion.

The plagues of frogs, gnats and flies.

The envoys of Jehovah were told that the Pharaoh refused to let the Israelites return to their land of Canaan for fear of losing such a large and convenient labor force. Yet they kept on trying; they were prepared, at the request of the king, to perform the prodigious acts mentioned by Jehovah: Aaron stretched out his hand, holding the miraculous rod, over the rivers, canals and marshes: vast quantities of frogs promptly emerged and threatened to overrun the country. The Pharaoh, duly impressed, allowed the Hebrews to go into the desert to celebrate their cult, and, at the request of Moses, Jehovah caused the frogs to die. The next time the king refused to let his people go, Aaron struck with his rod the dust of the ground which then turned into myriads of gnats; later on he caused swarms of flies to invade the country from the marshes.

ione
e ubu
ubus.
q eas
vides
ngra
. sic
n. Lo
tuaz
s inu
a. Ex
nens
uifes
re u
ypti.
tatio
io po
hoib.
phoez.
e cor
epat
moy
aam
ias:
inus.

... in ... populum ... 81

sus moyses a pharaone: orauit dominum qui fe
cit iuxta uerbum illius. et abstulit muscas
a pharaone et a seruis et a populo eius. et non superfuit
nec una quidem. Et ingrauatum est cor pharaonis. ita ut nec quidem hac uice dimitteret populum:

Dixit autem dominus ad moysen. Ingredere ad pharaonem et lo- IX
quere ad eum. Hec dicit dominus deus hebre-
orum. Dimitte populum meum ut sacrificet mi.

THE DEATH OF THE FIRSTBORN.

The nine plagues sent by Jehovah did not bend the will of the Pharaoh. So the Creator decided to send one last and terrible plague: in one single night he would put to death all the firstborn of the Egyptians and of their livestock while the Hebrews, having first marked their houses with the blood of slaughtered animals to distinguish them from those of the Egyptians, were celebrating a divinely prescribed sacrifice thereafter known as the Passover. Dawn on the following day was greeted with cries of heart-rending grief: not one family had been spared by the hand of Jehovah. The sight of so many dead bodies at last impressed on the king the will of the Creator. He thus summoned Moses and Aaron, ordered them to assemble the Hebrew people with all their possessions and urged them to leave the country where they had lived for four hundred and thirty years.

The crossing of the Red Sea.

Jehovah guided the Hebrews towards the shores of the Red Sea, appearing by day as a pillar of cloud and by night as a pillar of fire. They had reached the sea when the army of the Pharaoh, which had been sent to recover this valuable labor force, came into sight in the distance. On hearing murmurings of discontent among the multitudes Moses reassured his people, for he knew that Jehovah would not abandon them. While the Angel made a pillar of cloud between the Hebrews and their pursuers Moses ordered the waves to part so as to allow him and his followers to cross the sea on dry land. No sooner had they reached the other side than the Egyptians rushed into the opening; whereupon Moses, with outstretched hand, had the waters close over them.

inducam in te · ego enim sum dominus
sanator tuus. Venerunt autem filii isrl'
in helym ubi erant · xii · fontes aquarum et sep
tuaginta palme · et castrametati sunt iuxta
aquas; Profectique sunt de helym · et venit
omnis multitudo filiorum isrl' in desertum
sin · quod est inter helym et synay · quintodecimo
die mensis secundi · postquam egressi sunt de terra
egypti :·

XVI

Et murmuravit omnis congregatio fi
liorum isrl' contra moysen et aaron · in so
litudine: dixeruntque ad eos filii isrl' · uti
nam mortui fuissemus per manum domini in terra
egypti · quando sedebamus super ollas carni
um · et comedebamus panem in saturita
te · Cur eduxistis nos in desertum istud · ut

The miracles of the manna and the quails.

Starving in the desert, the Hebrews soon came to miss their years in Egypt where, even in servitude, they had always had enough bread and meat to eat. They began to murmur against Jehovah, though he clearly could not abandon them in this new scene of desolation in which both they and their livestock were in grave danger. At dusk he sent them flights of quails; then, the following morning, the Hebrews would find under the abundant dewdrops a heavenly bread, manna, which had the form of small grains and the taste of honey. For six days they built up reserves of this food and, on the seventh, celebrated their sabbath with a day of compulsory rest.

The Ten Commandments.

The Israelites had reached the Sinai desert and pitched their tents at the foot of Mount Sinai. From the top of the mountain Jehovah summoned his spokesman, Moses, instructing him to remind his people of the terms of the Covenant by which they were bound and the good things which had come their way since their departure from Egypt. He then told him to come up the mountain, alone, within two days. At daybreak the crowd of the Hebrews, in festive dress, knelt at the foot of the mountain, taking care not to go beyond the sacred limit which had been indicated to them. The top of Mount Sinai was hidden behind a dense layer of cloud; the sky was filled with thunder and lightning. Alone, Moses went up to the summit, where Jehovah, in a highly charged atmosphere, entrusted him with the Ten Commandments.

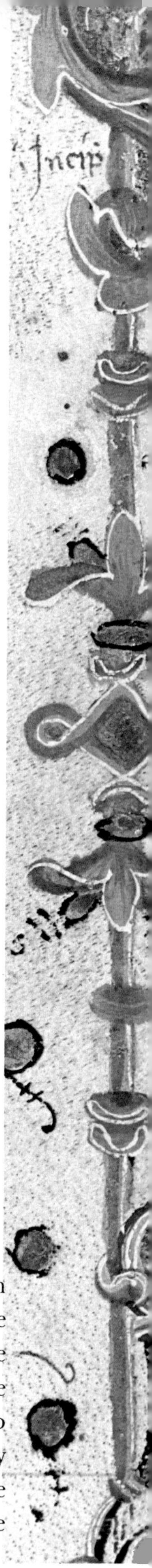

THE BUILDING OF THE TABERNACLE.

Moses spent forty days and forty nights face to face with Jehovah, deep in the cloud which covered the top of the mountain. From his lips he received the laws which were to govern the Covenant and the lives of the chosen people. He then described to him the offerings which he expected from the people and asked him to take charge of the building of the Tabernacle where the priests, surrounded by the people, would assemble in order to worship him. Having returned to his people waiting below, Moses conveyed to them the orders of Jehovah, whereupon many workers set about the task. On a hilltop they erected the four pillars in the middle of which the Ark of the Covenant was to stand and spread out above it the awning which was to protect the sacred dwelling and its riches from the wind and the sun.

[illegible] manebāt i eodē loco· nubes quip
pē dn̄i icubabat p diez tab'naclo· ⁊ ig's in
nocte· uidētib' pplis isrl' p cunctas mansiões suas·

Explic̄ lib' exodi· Incipit liber leuitici·

Uocauit aut̄ moysē· ⁊ locutus ē ei dominus d
tab'naculo testimonij dicens· Loquere

III. LEVITICUS

MOSES AT THE SANCTUARY *(previous page).*

From his towering cloud Jehovah had summoned Moses, who knelt before the sanctuary, his hands joined to receive the Lord's orders. The celestial Voice then dictated to him the whole ritual of offerings—burnt offerings, peace offerings, sin sacrifices and other forms of sacrifice—which the people of Israel would be required to observe, that same people which was already coming up towards the altar with their sacrificial animals, large and small, at their sides.

THE CONSECRATION OF THE PRIESTS *(above).*

Before the community which had gathered at the entrance to the sanctuary, Moses led forward his brother Aaron, followed by his sons. After performing the ritual ablutions on them he clad them in the priestly vestments; then, approaching his brother, he poured over his head the holy oil of anointing before laying his hands upon him. He proceeded in

a similar manner with each of the sons of Aaron, while the servants outside were preparing the bull which was to be immolated in order to atone for all the sins of Israel.

IV. NUMBERS

THE OFFERINGS OF THE PRINCES OF ISRAEL.

Moses had finished setting up the Tabernacle; he had also anointed and consecrated it, as well as the altar on which the fat of the sacrifical animals was to burn, and also the objects of the sacred cult. The crowned princes, the heads of the patriarchal families who had presided over the census, then came forward bringing with them their offerings: six covered wagons and twelve fat oxen. Moses received them outside the sanctuary and ordered them to deliver their gifts to the Levites for the service of the tent of assembly. Moreover, every day, one of the princes was to make his offering for the dedication of the altar: cups of fine flour and incense, and various animals, bulls, rams, and year-old lambs for the sacrifices of the burnt offering, the sin offering and the peace offering.

MOSES TALKS TO THE SONS OF REUBEN AND GAD.

The Hebrews had left the Sinai, led by the Ark of the Covenant and the cloud with which Jehovah guided them on their way. When they had reached the point agreed on by Moses and Aaron the huge caravan stopped; the Tabernacle was erected and they gave thanks to Jehovah for the manna and the quails which he had sent every day to the starving tribes. This did not mean, however, that each one of them followed the chosen route and kept to the instructions which had been given when they had begun their journey. Not a day went by without some revolt or rumbling of discontent alternating with manifestations of the divine anger and the prayers of Moses. For example, the sons of Reuben and Gad were refusing to press on towards Canaan. In the region of Jazer and Gilead they had found lush pastures for their flocks and were afraid to drive them further on towards more arid parts.

V. DEUTERONOMY

MOSES ADDRESSES HIS PEOPLE.

The trumpets had sounded in each of the tribes of Israel in order to stop all work and summon the people to a meeting on a treeless hill in the midst of the desert. Moses, whose words were inspired by Jehovah and whose voice thus became loud and authoritative, told his people of the divine message and the laws and customs which they, by virtue of the eternal Covenant concluded in the thunder of Mount Horeb, were obliged to follow. The powerful sound of his words was enhanced by the gestures which he made with his rod; the mediator of the Hebrews now had the authority which he needed to be their faithful guide.

VI. THE BOOK OF JOSHUA.

JOSHUA'S APPEAL.

Moses, now more than a hundred years old, had not reached his land of Canaan, the land promised to Abraham, Isaac and Jacob. He had only caught a glimpse of it from the top of Mount Nebo, where Jehovah had met him alone to inform him of his approaching death. After thirty days of mourning, the new guide called by God was Joshua, the faithful one. It was he who was to head the army of Israel as it crossed the Jordan on its way to the conquest of this vast country. Having been sent ahead as a spy by Moses, Joshua was already quite familiar with the long-sought after land of milk and honey, whose idolatrous inhabitants bowed before painted images and statues of molten metal.

The death of Joshua and the battle against the Canaanites.

After living the life of nomads for forty years in the desert, the Hebrews, as soon as they entered Canaan, suddenly turned into conquerors who thought of nothing besides fighting, plunder and slaughter. Notwithstanding the frequent discord among the tribes Joshua had managed to unite them into a single force which he then hurled against both north and south; Jehovah gave them his powerful assistance by causing the walls of the fortress-city of Jericho to come tumbling down, stopping the sun in order to allow the Hebrews to charge in pursuit, and sending a devastating hailstorm down on their enemies. Exhausted by so much warfare, Joshua handed over the conquered land to the tribes; then, with his dying words, he warned his people against idolatry.

THE MURDER OF SISERA.

Joshua's fears came true: his descendants worshipped idols and paid scant heed to the Judges. Jehovah, in his anger, delivered them to their enemies, the most ferocious of whom was Sisera, the chief of the Canaanite army. In despair the Israelites, acting on the advice of the prophetess Deborah, entrusted their destiny to Barak, who assembled their army on Mount Tabor. Sweeping down the mountain slopes he took his enemies by surprise on the plain and crushed them. Sisera, who had been unhorsed, fled shamefully on foot and took refuge in the tent of Jael. She hid him under a carpet and, when he was asleep, she hammered a tent stake through his temple so violently that the stake was driven into the ground. His pursuers soon appeared and Jael handed over Sisera's body.

GIDEON CROSSES THE JORDAN WITH THREE HUNDRED ISRAELITES.

No sooner had Deborah and Barak praised Jehovah in a victory hymn than the Hebrews slipped back into idolatry and once more incurred the divine anger. In order to escape from the Midianites they fled to the mountains where they lived in caves and cracks in the rocks. It was then that Jehovah, moved to pity, sent them Gideon, the master of devious strategy. Inspired by Jehovah, he chose the best three hundred soldiers of Israel and had them go at night to surround the enemy camp; each of them carried an empty pitcher containing a lamp and also a trumpet. Between them they made such a din that the enemy panicked, starting killing each other and fled. Driven onwards by an irresistible urge, he then took his hungry and tired men across the Jordan in pursuit of the Midianites.

SAMSON, DELILAH AND THE GATES OF GAZA.

The Hebrews had turned once more to their false gods and Jehovah, to punish them, delivered them to the Philistines. A giant, Samson of Nazareth, rose up against the occupying forces; he was filled with a desire for vengeance against those who had subjugated the country. One evening in Gaza it was rumored that he had gone into the house of a courtesan; an ambush was promptly set at the gates of the city in order to seize him. But to no avail! At dawn the giant forced his way through and returned to his refuge, taking with him both panels of the city gates. Shortly afterwards he fell in love with Delilah, a woman in the pay of the Philistines. Deploying the full measure of her charms she persuaded him to reveal the secret of his strength: his abundant hair. Samson, tired after a night of love-making, went to sleep on her knees; when he next awoke he found that his skull had been shaved smooth and he was powerless. His enemies then seized him with ease.

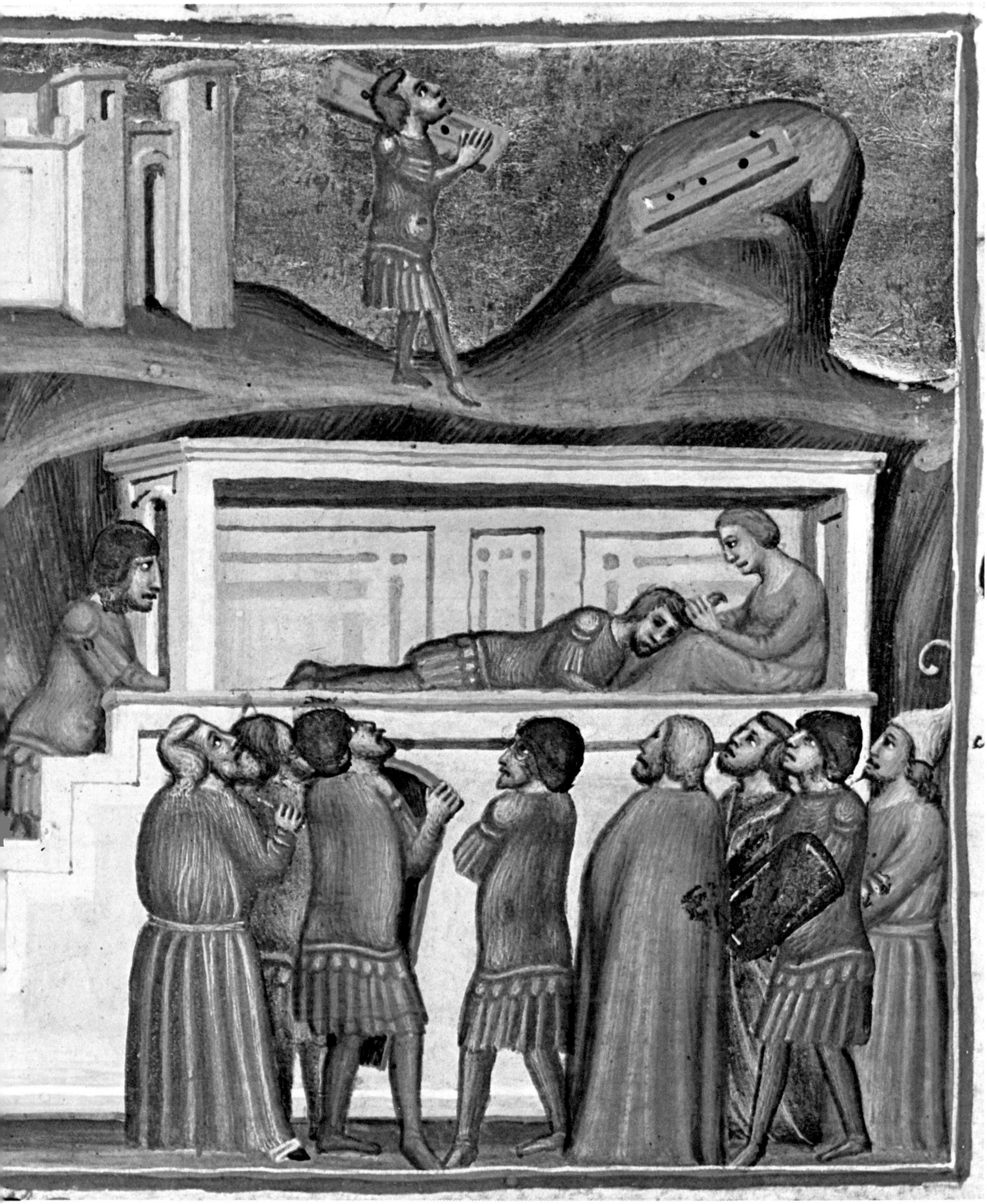

VIII. THE BOOK OF RUTH

ELIMELECH WITH HIS WIFE NAOMI AND HIS TWO SONS, MAHLON AND CHILION.

The reign of the Judges meant for Israel nothing but an unbroken series of conflicts full of cruelty, treachery and slaughter during which the people paid dearly for their infidelity to Jehovah. The extreme insecurity of this situation was heightened by famine; Elimelech, seeing his fields dried up or pillaged, decided to abandon his village of Bethlehem with his wife Naomi and his two sons. He reached the land of Moab where farming was good and where, once peace had returned, his heirs married two local women, Orpah and the virtuous Ruth who, when she became a widow, later returned to the land of Judah and married Boaz the reaper.

IX. THE FIRST BOOK OF KINGS

Elkanah and his two wives, Hannah and Peninnah.

Each year, the wise man Elkanah took his family on the ritual pilgrimage to the temple of Shiloh to worship Jehovah, the god of armies, and particularly to seek peace of mind for his two wives, Hannah, his favorite, and Peninnah, who, having borne him eight sons, cruelly mocked her barren rival. The high priest noticed a woman engaged in such intense prayer that she seemed to be drunk: her lips were moving constantly but silently. He went up to her and told her to go and sleep off her drunken excesses elsewhere; then he realized that she was crying because she could not bear her husband a child. Jehovah heard her prayer and, shortly after she returned home, Hannah gave birth to Samuel.

VICTORY OF THE ISRAELITES OVER THE PHILISTINES NEAR BETHCAR.

Having been abandoned by Jehovah, the idolatrous Israelites had to abandon the Ark of the Covenant in the hands of the Philistines until they, in turn, having been stricken by a series of plagues, were obliged to return it. Samuel the Judge saw in these signs proof of Jehovah's forgiveness; he therefore assembled the people for a long penitential fast and invited them to make a burnt offering of a lamb. The Philistine chiefs were disturbed on hearing of this new unity and were about to attack when a storm prevented them from moving: their soldiers were frightened by the flashes of lightning and panicked. Led by Samuel, the Israelites chased them as far as the boundaries of their country, at a point which was soon marked by a stone, in memory of the victory of Bethcar.

DAVID AND GOLIATH.

Saul, the first king of the Hebrews, turned away from Jehovah who then stripped him of his power. Samuel searched the whole country for a new monarch and discovered in Bethlehem a young shepherd called David who was capable of charming all those who heard him with the sounds of his harp. The old prophet promptly anointed him with oil from the sacred horn, thus giving the young man the spirit of Jehovah and the courage to confront the giant Goliath, who had come from the ranks of the Philistine army which was massed to face the Israelites. Wearing a helmet of brass and a coat of mail, the monster brandished his lance at the puny young man who had come forward armed only with a shepherd's staff, a sling and five stones. To everyone's surprise David felled the Philistine with a single stone between the eyes, after which he sliced off his head with his own sword.

persequuti philisteos usq; dum venirent
in vallem et usq; ad portas accaron

Cecideruntq; vulnerati de philisthijm in
in via salim usq; geth · et usq; accaron · Et
revertentes filij isrl postq fuerant p[er]secuti phi
listeos · invaserunt castra eor · Assumens

The deaths of Saul and Jonathan.

Although they frequently incurred the wrath of Jehovah, Saul and his son Jonathan spent their lives fighting the enemies of Israel and the dissidents, led by David, until the battle of Gilboa. The Israelites found themselves cornered and suffered heavy losses; Saul saw his three sons fall one after another. Fearing the force of his lance the enemy soldiers kept their distance and their archers showered so many arrows over him that one of them eventually lodged in his body. Knowing that he was seriously wounded, he asked his squire to pierce his heart with his own sword, so that he should not fall into the hands of the uncircumcised. Seeing that his worthy servant was hesitating to do his bidding, he flung himself on his sword and died.

The Amalekite carrying Saul's crown and bracelet is put to death on David's orders.

David had just conquered the Amalekites. While he was resting in his royal tent, he was told of the arrival of a young man, much the worse for wear, who claimed to have escaped from the terrible battle in which Saul had died. He was brought before the king, bowed low and confessed that he had fled from the battlefield; he also said that he, the Amalekite, had acceded to the request of the valiant Saul, who had been taken ill and could not fight on, and killed him. He laid on the ground Saul's crown and bracelet, as proof of his claim. All those present tore their clothes and fasted until nightfall in mourning. But David, finding the young fugitive's boasting highly suspicious, had him put to death by a stab in the neck for not having respected the Lord's chosen one.

David's victory over the Moabites.

Despite the spirit of revolt and vengeance which so gravely hampered the unity of the tribes of Israel, David conducted his military compaigns against all the enemies of the country. His sometimes bestial cruelty was matched only by the excesses of his opponents. Had he not just defeated the Moabites? He had the survivors of the vanquished army brought before him, behind whole cartloads of booty. He then ordered them to lie down in three rows; he measured them with a string and had the two outer rows put to death. As for those in the middle, he spared their lives on condition that they declared themselves to be his subjects and pay him tribute.

The death of Absalon.

David's family life was often marred by scandals, rapes and murders, amongst his many children. His favorite, Absalon, even arranged a conspiracy, which reached throughout the whole

of the state of Israel, against him. David had to leave his palace with those of his guards who had remained faithful. Absalon's army was beaten and the arrogant upstart put to flight. But David begged his commanders to spare his son's life. Imagine his grief when he learnt of the tragic outcome of the battle: the fugitive's steed had galloped under a big oak tree as he fled from his pursuers. Absalon's long hair, however, got caught on a branch, and the soldiers found him dangling there, ran him through and tossed his body into a ditch in the forest.

Ahab's victory over the Syrians *(following page)*.

The idolatrous king Ahab was for many years the object of the divine wrath. The whole of Israel had fallen on hard times; there was no more dew or rain, and the sea wind, bearing clouds, would not blow again until Ahab, converted by the prophet Elijah, eventually had his ministers of Baal put to death. Feeling that he now had the divine right on his side, he moved to expel the

buisti. et pugnabimus contra eos in campestribus. et videbitis quod obtinebimus eos. Credidit consilio eorum et fecit ita.

XXI

Igitur postquam annus transierat. recensuit Benadab syros. et ascendit in afech. ut pugnaret contra israel. Porro filii israel recensiti sunt. et acceptis cibariis profecti ex adverso. castraque metati sunt contra eos quasi duo parvi greges caprarum. syri autem repleverunt terram. Et ascendens unus vir dei. dixit ad regem israel. Hec dicit dominus. Quia

lem
bic
ei
mu
fac
tul
sita
fac
cap
Si
aia
mis
thr
atq
Et
g
nu
stu
tea
nis
Pe
qda
Inf
pcu
cem
leo
ni

fierce mountain warriors, the Syrians, from the land. For seven days the two armies camped face to face; his army looked more like a flock of goats, whereas that of the Syrians was heavily armed. Right, however, was with Ahab. The battle commenced; against all the odds, the Israelites were totally victorious. The Syrian survivors fled, taking refuge in the city of Aphek, where Jehovah caused the ramparts to fall in on them.

THE ILLNESS OF KING AHAZIAH.

Under the reign of Ahaziah the land of Judah was a prey to insecurity and was invaded by the Moabites. The young king was determined to fight them. However, one day, he fell from a balcony in his residence and was seriously injured. He sent for some of his relatives and had them consult the god Baal to find out whether or not he would get better, Jehovah sent the prophet to intercept them; he persuaded them to turn back, instead of going on to the oracle, and sent them back to the king. Ahaziah was furious and promptly dispatched a squad of soldiers to seize the prophet. Jehovah destroyed this force, and the one sent after it, by fire from heaven. In his bitterness Ahaziah eventually received the prophet who, at his bedside, reproached him for his idolatry and condemned him to die.

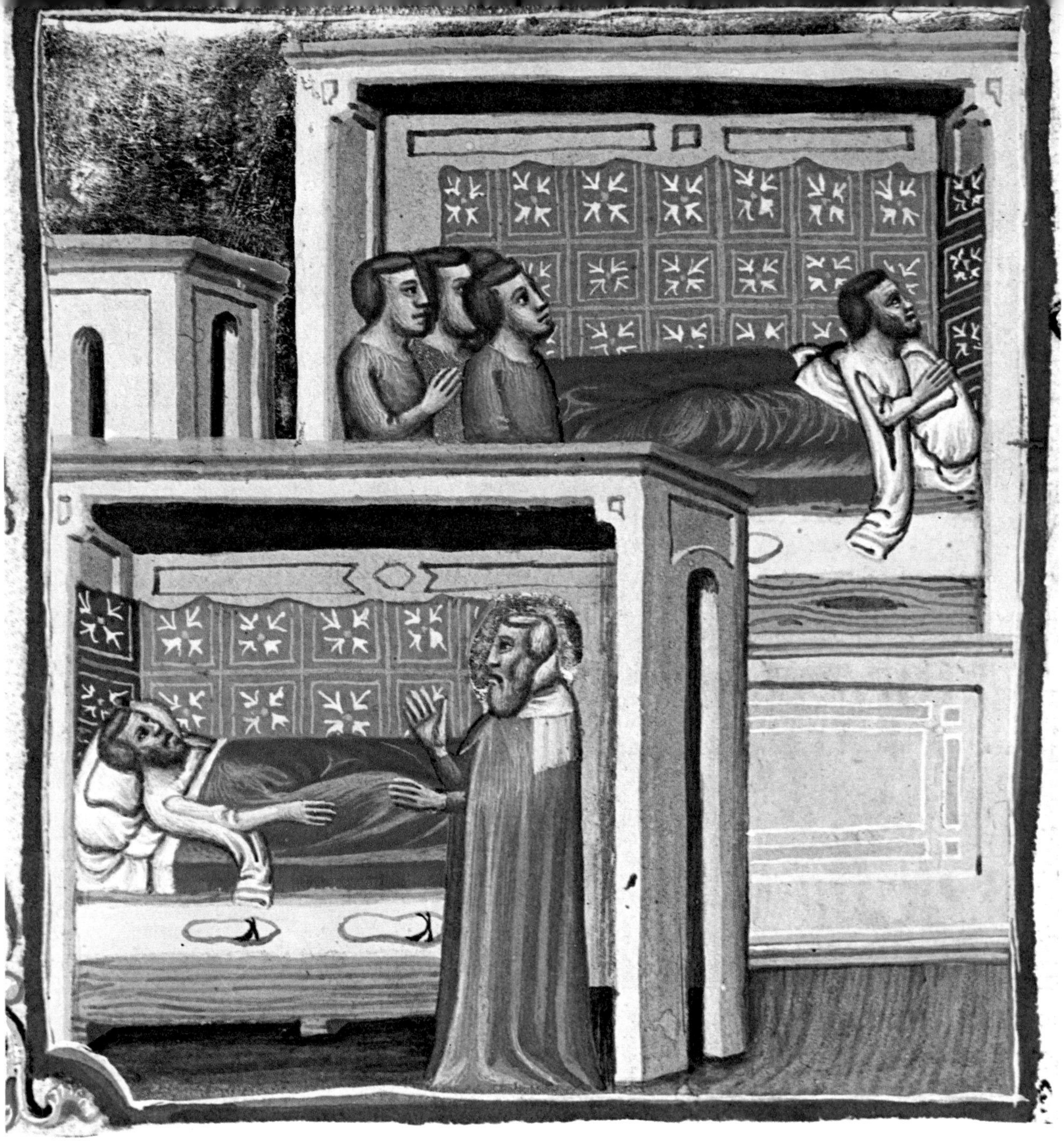

King Hezekiah.

Hezekiah ruled over the land of Judah. Obeying the orders of Jehovah he destroyed the false gods, burnt their temples and hunted down their priests. He was about to defeat the Assyrians when he was taken seriously ill. Isaiah was sent to see him as he lay dying and urged him to make a will. Hezekiah, in despair, pleaded with Jehovah to reward his fidelity by prolonging his life until he had had time to defeat the enemies of Judah. His wishes were granted, and the prophet applied to the boil which was sapping his strength a cake of figs. Three days later the king was well enough to go to the temple to give thanks to Jehovah and recover, at the foot of the altar, the strength he needed to expel the Assyrians from the country.

X. THE BOOK OF CHRONICLES.

THE DREAM OF SOLOMON.

After forty years of conflict and intrigue, David had reunited the kingdoms of Israel under his rule; his life ended happily, in the midst of honors and riches. His son Solomon succeeded him. The first act of his reign was a sacrifice, in Jerusalem, of a thousand burnt offerings to Jehovah in the presence of the officers, judges and princes of Israel. On the night which followed the ceremony Jehovah appeared to him in his sleep and asked him what he wanted. The young king replied that he hoped he would give him the wisdom and the knowledge necessary in order to govern the very large people of Israel. Jehovah was so impressed by his common sense that he promised him, in addition, riches and glory, because he had not actually asked for those things.

Israelite horsemen drive out the Ethiopians under King Asa.

Asa, king of Judah, took new measures against the disciples of Baal, in keeping with the wishes of Jehovah; he had the statues and altars erected by the foreigners smashed to pieces. Taking advantage of the peace prevailing in the country he consolidated his power by building fortified cities with huge ramparts and reorganizing his army. This reform had been scarcely concluded when the kingdom was invaded by a band of black Ethiopians wearing turbans, with war chariots. With the aid of Jehovah the soldiers of Israel routed them, destroying their chariots and pursuing them beyond the frontier. After a campaign of looting and massacres Asa's army returned to Jerusalem laden with riches, while numerous flocks of sheep and camels brought up the rear.

XI. THE BOOK OF EZRA

Nehemiah

These who had survived captivity in Babylon took advantage of the leniency of the successors of Nebuchadnezzar and returned to Jerusalem. Cyrus and Artaxerxes, the king of Persia, decided to rebuild the city, its ramparts and temple with the aid of the Hebrews. Among them, on their return to the land of Judah after twelve years of exile, was Nehemiah, the royal cup-bearer. Invoking the law of Moses as expounded by the scribe Ezra, he addressed the crowd assembled at the Water Gate, asking them to forget the great grief which they had experienced, to seek new strength in Jehovah and to celebrate the holy day in renewed joy by rejoicing in the prescribed manner.

et salmias · et nathan · et adaias · mechne-
dabei · sisay · sarai · ezrel · et selemau · sere-
mia · sellum · amaria · ioseph · De filiis
nebu iahel · mathathias · zaleth · et
zabina · ieddu · iohel · banaia ·
Omnes hy acceperant alienenas · et
fuerunt ex his mulieres que peperant
filios :- Explic. primus liber esdre. Incip. ii.

Verba neemie filii helchie · et factum est
in mense casleu in anno uicesimo .
et ego eram in susis castro · Et uenit ana-
ni unus de fratribus meis ipse et uiri iuda ·
et interrogaui eos de iudeis qui remanse-
rant et superant de captiuitate et de ierusalem .
Et dixerunt michi · Qui remanserunt et relicti

King Josiah

Josiah, who had become king while still a child, observed the law passed down by Moses and complied with the teachings of his scribes, priests and levites. No sooner had he reached the age of adulthood than he undertook to rid Judah and Jerusalem of the graven and molten images of false gods, using fire to do so. He made dust of them and strewed it over the tombs of the dead idolaters. In order to restore the former glory of the dwelling-place of Jehovah he decided that thenceforth the gold and silver offered in sacrifice would be distributed to the masons and carpenters so that they could go out and buy stone and structural timber. Then, having re-opened the book of the Law, he won back to the Covenant those who had strayed from it and handed out the meat of lambs and oxen for the Passover.

Ezra, the scribe versed in the Law of Moses and a favorite of the king of Persia, Artaxerxes, had returned to Jerusalem with a crowd of Jews laden with gifts and produce which the treasurers of the kingdom had given them: wheat, wine, oil and salt. They also brought with them bulls, rams and lambs which were to be sacrificed to Jehovah by their priests according to the prescribed ritual. However, in Jerusalem, Ezra was laid low by calamitous news which had been brought to him and promptly began to fast as a sign of his grief: the people, the priests and even the levites had, it seemed, sullied the blood of the chosen people by taking foreign wives. With the help of Jehovah he warned all sinners to recover their former purity and to expel these unworthy creatures together with all their offspring.

XII. THE BOOK OF TOBIAS

TOBIAS THE ELDER

Tobias of Galilee had been in captivity in Nineveh where, together with his wife Hannah and his young son, his life had been spent offering the first fruits and tithes to Jehovah, while at the same time distributing to his indigent brothers the little worldly wealth which was still his. The ageing king of Assyria, Salmanasar, became his protector, authorized him to move about the country and continue his charitable work among the captives. Tobias handed out alms, clothed those who were naked and, in particular, buried the numerous dead bodies which marked the passage of the new king Sennacherib. The royal police failed to catch him, as he had taken refuge with some friends who had him in a safe place; in this way be continued to bury the dead until the unfortunate day when, as he lay resting from his labors under a tree, a swallow's droppings happened to fall on his eyes, blinding him.

XIII. THE BOOK OF JUDITH

VICTORY OF NEBUCHADNEZZAR OVER ARPHAXAD, KING OF THE MEDES.

Arphaxad, king of the Medes, had swept through the Orient at the head of his batallions of mercenaries and his war chariots. He had vanquished many nations and had built a fortress city made of squared blocks of stone, surrounded by huge ramparts and towers. The king of Assyria, Nebuchadnezzar, was none too happy with the presence of such a dangerous neighbor; so he sought allies and managed to lure Arphaxad into a great plain where his soldiers, all of them from the mountains, were routed in the midst of huge clouds of dust.

THE BEHEADING OF HOLOPHERNA

Nebuchadnezzar took a terrible and bloody revenge, sending out his general Holopherna at the head of a formidable army of chariots, horsemen and archers. In sheer terror, the kings and princes in his path sent ambassadors to meet him, the tribes came towards him submissively with crowns, flaming torches and dancing. But Holopherna turned a deaf ear to their appeals, and destroyed town after town. As the killing continued, he arrived at the gates of Bethulia, in Israel, where the rich and beautiful Judith lived alone, a widow. She was tired of hearing the elders lamenting, so, invoking the aid of Jehovah, she made ready for the trip and, accompanied by a single lady in waiting she went to Holopherna's camp. The general, suitably impressed by both her wisdom and her beauty, invited her to stay for dinner. Having drunk copiously at the table he fell into a deep sleep—whereupon Judith seized his sword which was hanging from a tentpole and sliced off his head, which she then took back in a bag to her people in Bethulia.

The dinner party of King Ahasuerus

The lands under the control of King Ahasuerus stretched all the way from India to Ethiopia. From his magnificent palace at Susa, his capital city, he dispatched messengers to the governors and generals of all his provinces inviting them to a banquet. For more than a hundred days Ahasuerus displayed before their eyes all the splendors of his kingdom and entertained them all until they had had their fill of the choicest foods, wines and all manner of festivities. He then assembled all the men of his capital and invited them to a banquet which lasted seven days; in the midst of exquisite drapes and pillars of marble and porphyry he regaled them with wine from the royal cellars, served in golden goblets. Meanwhile, Queen Vasthi gave a similar banquet for the women. His heart gladdened by protracted rounds of drinking, the king sent his eunuchs to beg her to come and join him; yet she was most offended to find that his invitation was being extended to her by the likes of them, so she refused to come, whereupon the king flew into a rage.

XV. THE BOOK OF JOB

Job

Not far from the Dead Sea lived a man of great integrity called Job who, through fear of Jehovah, took care to avoid any form of evil. He lived a peaceful nomadic life in the midst of his flocks of sheep camels, oxen and donkeys, watching over his seven sons and three daughters; he was particularly anxious to preserve the purity of his offspring, so he had them cleanse themselves by means of a sacrifice each time they had taken part in festivities of any sort. But one day bands of enemy soldiers, allied to the fire of heaven and that of the desert, swooped down on his property and destroyed his flocks and his family. Griefstricken, Job tore his garments, shaved his head, prostrated himself on the ground and said: "Naked I came from my mother's loins, and naked I shall return there. May the name of Jehovah be blessed!".

XVI. SALOMON'S BOOK OF PROVERBS

KING SOLOMON

Solomon, the son of David and king of Israel, dictated to his scribes a series of proverbs the purpose of which was to give the young the wisdom and mental discipline which they needed in order to know the truth and act with justice. The reader of the Proverbs is invited, for example, to avoid the company of the wicked, to distrust strange women, whose lips drip honey, to imitate the diligent and prudent ant and, above all, to steer clear of the seven abominations: haughty eyes, the lying tongue, criminal hands, the heart which thinks of ways to do evil, feet which are drawn towards wickedness, false witnesses and trouble-makers.

Solomon the Preacher

His sword in his right hand, and the scales of justice in his left, Solomon the Wise, the Preacher, addressed an assembly of the Jews reminding them that on earth all is vanity, as the generations succeed one another whereas the sun, the wind and the rivers live on unchanged. He spoke of the vanity of wisdom, of human pleasure, of the strivings of man against the force of events or the tyranny of those in power, and of the death which inexorably follows all of these things. He spoke of the hardships of life on earth: the oppression of the weak, the vanity of competition, the coldness of the lonely life, the goad of politics, religious routine and the tyranny of power. There was, he proclaimed, only one way to avoid all these things: to yield to Jehovah's providence.

ISAIAH

In a prophetic vision—fitting for a man who had seen Jehovah in the Tabernacle—Isaiah uttered a series of oracles against the ungrateful people who had turned away from Jehovah, against the inhabitants of Sodom and Gomorrah, who were wallowing in perversion. He lamented over Jerusalem, the faithful City, a prey to murderers, rebels, drunkards and whores "with tinkling rings on their feet". He saw the punishments which were to come hurtling down on the city which had not heeded the call of Jehovah from the top of the holy mountain. Then, once the storm had passed, he finally announced the awakening of Jerusalem and its recovery from plunder and ruin, after it had found justice and peace under the guidance of the Messiah.

Jeremiah

The prophetic voice of Jeremiah rang out over a Jerusalem which was enduring the scourge sent by God because it had broken the Covenant with Jehovah and persisted in living a life of hedonistic materialism and hardened cynicism which the Creator could not ignore. "They have set up their iniquity in the House which bears my name in order to desecrate it". Did this mean that the evil was incurable? Certainly not: Israel was the chosen land, and Jeremiah made it clear that, after due atonement had been made in the form of exile, captivity, siege and ruin, the eternal city of Jerusalem would be saved by the Messiah and would then find renewed glory which would make it the envy of all nations.

Baruch

The Babylonian exile had already lasted for many generations, and the Jews of the Diaspora celebrated the anniversary of the capture of Jerusalem by the Chaldaeans. Far from their fatherland they wept, fasted, prayed and collected money in the hope that the offerings and the sacrifices thus bought in Jerusalem would appease the wrath of Jehovah and make it possible, one day, for the homesick exiles to see once again the sacred hill on which their forefathers had celebrated the Covenant.

XXI. THE BOOK OF THE PROPHET EZEKIEL

THE VISION OF EZEKIEL

Ezekiel, the prophet of exile, having witnessed one of the most tragic episodes in the history of Israel, the fall of Jerusalem and the deportation of the Jews, had a dream one day on the banks of the Shobar. In an apocalyptic vision he saw, in the midst of a vast cloud, the chariot of Jehovah drawn by four strange animals with four faces and four wings, the bodies of lions and the hooves of oxen. The fantastic scene was suddenly illuminated by a bright glow and flashes of lightning, a sign of the heavenly glory which told Ezekiel that Jehovah, despite his anger, was still with his people, even if they were exiled in far-off Babylon.

tes senectas :- Explicit prologus
liber ezechielis prophete :-- I

factum ē · In tricesimo anno ī qr̄
mense in quinta mensis · cū eēt
io captiuor iux̄ fluuium chobar

XXII. THE BOOK OF THE PROPHET DANIEL

KING NEBUCHADNEZZAR AND THE FOUR CHILDREN OF THE ROYAL BLOOD: DANIEL, ANASIAS, MISAEL AND AZARIAS

Nebuchadnezzar, king of Babylon, had seized Jerusalem, plundering the city and removing the treasures of the House of God to the banks of the Euphrates. While he was in the capital of Judah he was struck by the good looks and the intelligence of some of the adolescents of the leading families there. Accordingly, no sooner had he returned to his palace, than he dispatched his chief eunuch to find those young people who were so accomplished in learning and so wise in their knowledge, with orders to bring them to his court where Chaldaean scholars would teach them the language and customs of the country. In this way, Daniel and his companions enjoyed the favor of the king for three years, while at the same time remaining faithful to the Jewish Law.

THE THREE YOUNG MEN IN THE FURNACE

Nebuchadnezzar had built a gold statue six cubits high on a plain near Babylon. On the royal orders the high officials of his kingdom had gathered at the foot of this idol and, to the sound of music, bowed low before it in adoration. However, some of the Chaldaeans, seeing that Daniel's three compannions refused to make such an idolatrous gesture, denounced them to the king. He promptly had a furnace made, seven times bigger than usual, tied up the young people and had them tossed into the flames. The heat of the fire was so great that the three executioners themselves were roasted alive. However, Ananias, Misael and Azarias were protected by an angel who came and untied their bonds; the three young men then knelt, unharmed, in the middle of the blaze, and blessed the name of the God of their fathers.

The story of Susanna

The following story is but one example of the turbulent human passions which marked the life of the Jews in their remote land of exile. Susanna, the wife of Joachim, was so stunningly beautiful that two old judges fell in love with her. Although they were supposed to be the guides of the people of Israel during their Babylonian exile, the two old men promptly forgot the Law of Jehovah and, following their instincts, tried to corrupt the virtue of the model wife as she was bathing in her garden. Only the wisdom of the young Daniel upset their false testimony, refuted them and caused them to be subjected to the punishment which had originally been intended for the chaste Susanna, whom the two jealous suitors had accused of having an affair with a young friend.

mui lauati sut. ad usus eam-
go ipsis cum festinatione.

senes. Venit et sedit in medio
a nob. qr tibi dedit deus lo

XXIII. THE BOOK OF THE PROPHET HOSEA

Hosea

During his long life, Hosea, the man of God, had known the five kings Uzziah, Jotham, Ahaz, Hezekiah and Jeroboam; despite the great tragedy which had befallen him within his own family, he never ceased to offer his wisdom to the great ones of this world. His prophecies dealt with the infidelity of the people of Israel which, like his wife Gomer who had become a prostitute, was wallowing in all manner of sexual excesses. Yet, his anger towards the woman who had left him was matched by his love for the mother of his three children; similarly Jehovah was ready to forgive the infidelity of those who had abandoned his Law.

XXIV. THE BOOK OF THE PROPHET JOEL

JOEL

Israel had just been struck by two plagues —locusts and drought. While the drunkards were stuffing themselves with wine, a horde of hungry insects was reducing the fig-trees, the vineyards, the ears of wheat and barley to the state of whitened skeletons; the drought, on the other hand, prevented the seeds from germinating, emptied the granaries and turned the pasture lands a brown color. In their distress the Jews turned to the prophet, whose advice to them was that they should fast and do penance in the hope that Jehovah, in his mercy, would annihilate the locusts and bring back over their land the rainclouds which would restore to the starving people their stocks of grain and their vats of wine and fresh oil.

prephacio. Incipit liber amos prophete. I.

Verba amos qui fuit in pastoralibus de thecue. que vidit super israel in diebus ozie regis iuda et in diebus ieroboam filii ioas regis israel. ante duos annos terremotus. Et dixit. Dominus de syon rugiet et de ierusalem dabit vocem suam. Et luxerunt speciosa pastorum. et exsiccatus est vertex carmeli. Hec dicit dominus. Super tribus sceleribus damasci et super quatuor non convertam eum. eo quod trituraverunt in plaustris ferreis galaad. Et mittam ignem in domo aza

usque in
man
Super
quatu
rit pre
timum
muro
latu i
tione
ipse i p
N
non au
regis
tam ig
noth
clang
de me
interfi
conv[er]
um. no
domu
rit. T
que a[l]
ignem
hec dic
israel
derunt

XXV. THE BOOK OF THE PROPHET AMOS

AMOS

During the reigns of Uzziah and Jeroboam II Israel enjoyed a long period of peace reminiscent of the glorious times of Solomon and David. Prosperity gave the well-to-do a taste for easy living, which then led to an endless round of banquets and orgies. Jehovah's anger manifested itself through a number of warning plagues, but the people of Israel took no heed. At this point a shepherd from Bethlehem, Amos, entered the picture. In a down-to-earth no-nonsense manner, he traveled through the offending cities, predicting, in a series of visions, the plagues which would be visited upon them; finally he spoke to them of the mysterious punishment which would make the sun set at noon and plunge Israel into desolation.

XXVI. THE BOOK OF THE PROPHET OBADIAH

OBADIAH

The vision of Obadiah was intended simply as a call for vengeance by the people of Israel against the Edomites, who had committed numerous acts of aggression; the time had come to form an armed alliance of all those who had suffered at their hands. This call for a holy war, which had the support of Jehovah, eventually made it possible to drive the warlike Edomites from their mountain retreats, to lay waste their territories, to make slaves of their survivors, and thus, on the day of Jehovah, to restore the splendor of the old Jerusalem.

JONAH FALLS INTO THE SEA

Jonah was instructed by Jehovah to go to Nineveh, the rich city on the banks of the Euphrates, to warn its inhabitants that the wickedness of the Babylonians could not go unnoticed by the eye of God. Shortly after he set sail the ship on which he was traveling was nearly destroyed by an extremely violent storm. The crew became frightened and jettisoned their valuable cargo, while Jonah sat quietly in the vessel's hold. It seemed certain to them that the cause of their misfortune was their strange passenger. Jonah, realizing that he had attracted the divine anger to the hapless ship, asked the men to throw him into the sea. Jehovah, however, arranged for him to be swallowed by an enormous fish and deposited on dry land, safe and sound, three days later.

XXVIII. THE BOOK OF THE PROPHET MICAH

MICAH

Micah, who came from a small village in Judea, lived during the reigns of Kings Jotham, Ahaz and Hezekiah, at a time when the power and prestige of Assur reached all the way to the kingdom of Judah, where the rich landowners were in constant conflict with the helpless poor peasants. The Jewish fraternity was now definitely a thing of the past. In a series of oracles, Micah leveled accusations against the arrogant Samarians and declared that their idols, which had been built with the earnings of prostitutes, would be destroyed. This prophet of doom and redemption also had harsh words for Israel: he foretold its ruin, but also implied that Jehovah might forgive it on the day when the walls of Jerusalem were rebuilt.

XXIX. THE BOOK OF THE PROPHET NAHUM

NAHUM

The tyrant of Assyria was heading inexorably for disaster; the once powerful Nineveh now found armies of Medes and Babylonians marching beneath its very walls; eventually they entered the city and turned its streets into scenes of carnage. At the sight of such severe retribution Nahum was delighted; he now felt there was a greater likelihood of peace and freedom for the land of Judah. The disappearance of a city such as Nineveh, poisoned by its false gods, but not before it had inflicted untold suffering upon the people of Israel, could not fail to be the fate which Jehovah held in store for all accursed cities which rebelled against his omnipotence.

gius · Incipit liber ·

XXX. THE BOOK OF THE PROPHET HABAKKUK

HABAKKUK

In a lengthy dialogue with Jehovah Habakkuk spoke on behalf of his people who had suffered at the hands of a bloodthirsty and impious invader. Jehovah was none too prompt in coming to the aid of those who, after all, were merely paying the price of their own treachery. But Habakkuk remained vigilant, denouncing the Chaldaeans at great length and in the strongest terms; at his request Jehovah promised an early delivrance to his people, now that the oppressor was proving to be so utterly bloodthirsty and treacherous.

XXXI. THE BOOK OF THE PROPHET ZEPHANIAH

ZEPHANIAH

The prophets had never been lacking in divine plagues with which to convey their message to the people; when the word of God was revealed to Zephaniah the masters of the land of Judah were the Assyrians. The court, the dignitaries and the entire Jewish nation seemed to have come to terms with the new cult of Baal, and trembled when the conquering legions marched past the city walls on their way to Egypt. In the seclusion of his silent retreat, the prophet Zephaniah, who was as deeply distressed by the conduct of his impious fellow Jews as he was by the plunderous forays of the occupying forces, eventually came forth and announced the Day of Jehovah, the cataclysm which was to engulf all the enemies of Israel and, together with them, even Israel itself if God did not waive the terrible sentence which hung over it.

quod conticuit omnis populus chanaan. et disperierunt
uniuersi qui inuoluti erant argento:

Explicit prologus. Incipit liber. I.

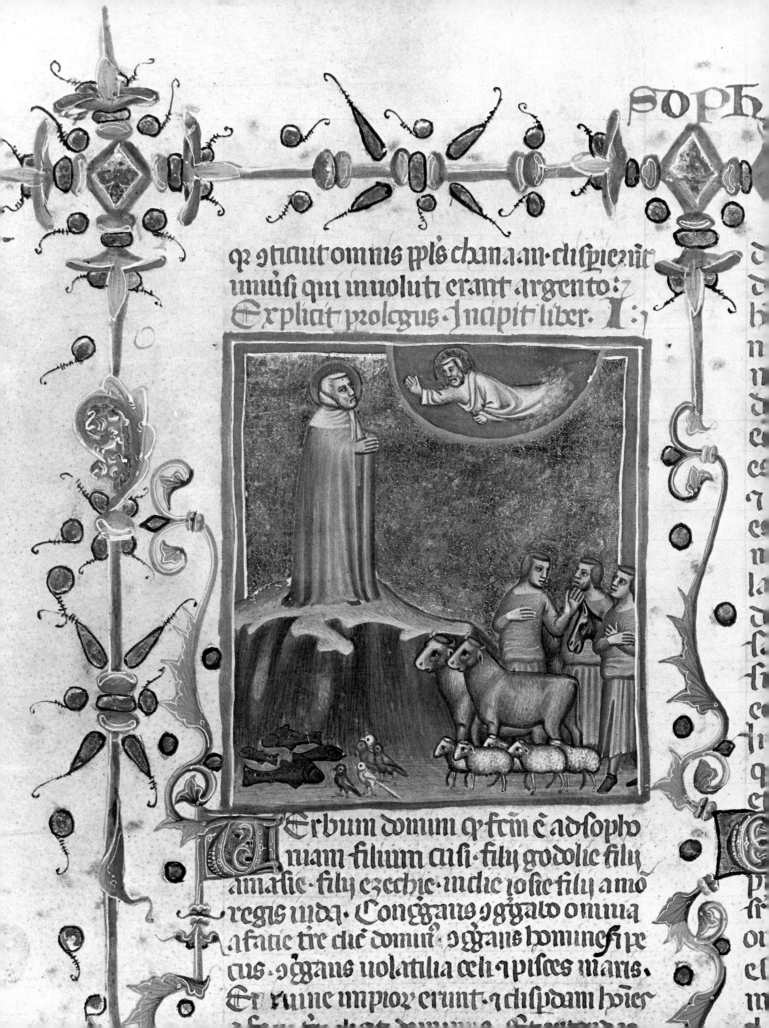

Verbum domini quod factum est ad sopho
niam filium cusi. filij godolie filij
amasie. filij ezechie. in die iosie filij amon
regis iude. Congregans congregabo omnia
a facie terre dicit dominus. congregans hominem et pe
cus. congregans uolatilia celi et pisces maris.
Et ruine impiorum erunt. et disperdam homines

XXXII. THE BOOK OF THE PROPHET HAGGAI

Haggai

Cyrus had allowed the Jews to return to their country, thus putting an end to their long captivity. They settled once more in Jerusalem, where their first concern was to rebuild the city walls, its Temple and the altar of burnt offerings. As they worked, however, they soon became discouraged by the lack of food resulting from a series of bad harvests and also by the unceasing attacks of the bandits who roamed the land looting as they went. At this moment the prophet Haggai intervened to bolster the courage of the faithful, urging them to press on with the reconstruction of the Temple, so that the spirit of Jehovah might live amongst them.

XXXIII. THE BOOK OF THE PROPHET ZECHARIAH

The visions of Zechariah

Among those who had returned from captivity in Babylon, Jehovah had chosen Zechariah in order to convey to him his divine message in a series of eight visions. Two of them presaged, in allegorical form, the rebuilding of the Tabernacle and the return of Israel to the faith of Moses. Before a stone tabernacle two angels held aloft the jars containing the oil which was to be used to anoint the future ministers and kings, while the seven-armed candelabra symbolizing the divine light appeared floating in the air. In the foreground the four celestial carriages passed by, the first two of them drawn by one russet and one white horse. Emerging from between the two brass mountains which marked the entrance to the abode of the Babylonian gods, the chariots then moved off in the direction of the four winds of heaven to announce the return of Jehovah.

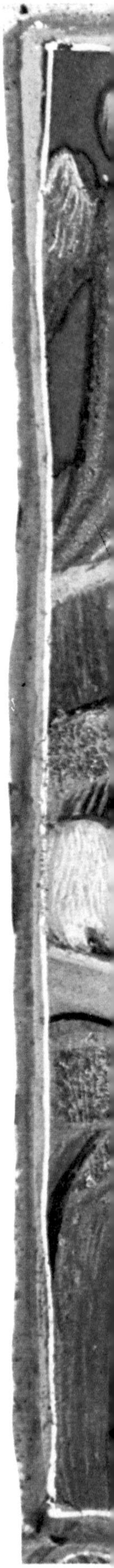

XXXIV. THE BOOKS OF MACCABEUS

Judas Maccabeus

Alexander the Great had pressed his conquests as far as the outer limits of the known world; Israel, too, had not been spared the influence of Hellenistic culture, with all its false gods and sacrilegious plunder. In the land of Judah, ever since the pagan Citadel had been erected opposite the Temple, a revolt had been brewing. Mattathias left Jerusalem with his sons, among them Judas Maccabeus, who led the fight against the invader. At the head of a handful of faithful he attacked Seron the general of the Syrian army, trusting in the help of Jehovah who would not abandon those who were fighting for their families, their laws and their country. Brandishing over his head the sword taken from the vanquished Appollonius, his first adversary, he swooped down upon the enemy, taking them by surprise, routing them and pursuing the survivors into the land of the Philistines.

JUDAS MACCABEUS AND NICANOR

The Roman usurper Demetrius had seized the throne of the Seleucids and resumed the fight against the Jews, who were still under the leadership of the intrepid Judas Maccabeus. The mission of destroying the people of Judah was entrusted to a general named Nicanor who was anxious to avenge an earlier defeat. Despite the great size of his army, Nicanor realized that sheer force would not make it possible for him to win, so he tried more devious means. Accompanied by only a small escort, clearly visible to all, he advanced to make peace overtures to the Jews, while his troops were massing in Jerusalem, ready to kidnap their leader. Judas Maccabeus, however, suspected a ruse and, instead of going to meet Nicanor, assembled his people for battle and won yet another victory.

THE DEATH OF JUDAS *(following page)*

Demetrius was furious when he learnt of the death of the defeated Nicanor and the alliance between the Jews and the military might of Rome. He resumed the attack on Jerusalem. Judas Maccabeus managed to assemble only a small force, which was soon intimidated by the size of the opposing army. His men began to panic. Eventually, however, he succeeded in gathering

together a small group of the faithful with whom he attacked the Syrian phalanxes of Bacchides, to the sound of trumpets. After the confrontations between the archers and the slingers, the cavalry charged but was dispersed by Judas Maccabeus; he failed to notice, however that enemy troops had encircled him from behind. Now finding themselves overwhelmed on all sides, his men took to their heels, and Judas himself was killed, his sword still in his hand.

The high priest Jonathan Maccabeus

Jonathan, the brother of Judas, was the new guide of the Hebrews as they were relentlessly pursued by Bacchides, the right-hand man of the cruel and treacherous upstart, Demetrius. Jonathan stood his ground, and, like his brother, returned blow for blow, with the result that the enemy eventually desisted and came to terms with Jerusalem. Alexander sought the friendship of Jonathan, appointed him high priest of the Jewish people and conferred upon him the purple chlamys and the crown of gold. On hearing of this, Demetrius dispatched another envoy to Jonathan, laden with gifts and promises: the Jews would be the masters of their own territory and could celebrate their religious festivals. Jonathan, however, chose to stay faithful to the pact he had concluded with Alexander.

The israelites save king Demetrius Nicator of Syria

Peace had been concluded between the high priest Jonathan and Demetrius Nicator of Syria, who had just established a new charter for the Jewish people. At Antioch the army had been sent back home, and the mercenaries, now finding themselves unemployed, turned against Demetrius and began to side with the son of Alexander, the rightful heir to the throne. Fearing a rebellion Demetrius renewed his promises to the high priest Jonathan and summoned him to his aid. The Jewish army took Antioch, and, having first assured the security of the king, they then went on a shameless rampage of killing and burning throughout the city. Triumphant and laden with gifts, the Israelites returned to Jerusalem, only to learn that none of the promises made by Demetrius would ever be kept.

The three brothers Maccabeus pursue the infidels

Apollonius, governor of Syria, had provoked Jonathan, the high priest of the mountain; in order to facilitate the movement of his cavalry, he then invited him to come down into the plain to do battle. Jonathan took up the challenge; in the company of Judas and Mathathias he charged at the infidels. The Hebrews foiled the crafty tactics of Apollonius, exhausting his cavalry by means of lengthy detours and opened enormous gaps in the enemy ranks. The infidels, by now thoroughly demoralised and in any case anxious to save their gold standard, fled on horseback, leaving behind them a number of towns which Jonathan would soon burn to the ground.

Victory of Jonathan Maccabeus over the army of Demetrius Nicator

Jonathan discovered that the generals of Demetrius Nicator, the king whose promises were false, were on their way at the head of a large army in order to strip him of his title of high priest. Leaving the country in the care of his brother Simon he set up his camp opposite that of the enemy force, in full view of everyone just in case an ambush was attempted. His precautions were to no avail, however, and Jonathan found himself abandoned by many of his troops. He was so deeply disappointed by such cowardice that he tore his clothing, covered himself with dust and started to pray. Upon seeing their leader's dignified anger express itself in this way, his men returned to the fray and swooped down on the enemy camp; they took it by storm and settled there, as the stragglers of the enemy force took to their heels.

Simon Maccabeus and his two sons, John and Judas

The high priest Jonathan, having been lured into a trap, had fallen into the hands of the enemy, who kept him as a hostage for a while and then put him to death. His successor was his brother Simon, who had also been reared for the post of high priest; various foreign princes, including both Demetrius and Antiochus, sought to ally themselves with him. One day, John warned his father that General Kendebea was marching on the land of Israel at the head of an army. The high priest, who was now quite old, promptly decided to place his two sons, John and Judas, at the head of the Israelites. John divided the army into two groups, led one of them across a stream and, to the sound of trumpets, took the enemy completely by surprise and put them to flight. Unfortunately his brother Judas was wounded in the fighting and could not take part in the pursuit.

Two Jewish messengers

Each year the Jewish people celebrated the feast of Tabernacles, in memory of the inauguration of the Temple of Jerusalem. On that occasion two messengers left the holy city and traveled to Egypt to visit their brothers who had stayed behind in that country to wish them peace and to remind them of the celebration of the feast, at which oxen and lambs were consumed on the altar by

the sacred flame. After all, was not the flame itself miraculous? When the Jews left Egypt at the time of the Exodus they had secretly placed the flame at the bottom of a dried up well; yet when they went back to look for it they found nothing but muddy water which, however, turned into a great purifying flame when it was brought into contact with the wood of the altar.

VICTORY OF THE ISRAELITES LED BY JUDAS MACCABEUS OVER THE SOLDIERS OF NICANOR

During the time of Antiochus Epiphanes, Judas Maccabeus assembled those who had remained faithful to Judaism in order to fight those who profaned the Temple and reconquer the country. One of the king's favorites, Nicanor, traveled throughout Israel in the hope of capturing Jews and then selling them as slaves at a price of ninety-nine to one talent, in order to pay off a tribute which he owed to the Romans. The terrified Jews fled in all directions; Judas appealed to them to stay calm, to join him and to wait until Jehovah gave them the strength to win. With the help of his

brothers he formed a number of armed groups which attacked and routed Nicanor's troops. Having looted the enemy camp, they then celebrated the Sabbath and distributed their booty among the widows, the poor and the orphans of their people.

JUDAS MACCABEUS AND THE ANGELS OF JEHOVAH.

The assistance of Jehovah sometimes took a very direct form on the battlefield; for instance, when Judas Maccabeus was fighting Timotheus, the enemy of his people, five shining angels appeared on horseback at the head of the Jewish army. Two of them formed a protective shield around Judas and hurled thunderbolts at the numerically superior enemy, blinding them and causing them to flee in panic. Timotheus took refuge in a fortress, but Judas, who was still guided by the envoys of Jehovah, laid siege to him there, set fire to the towers and captured the entire place. Timotheus who was eventually found hiding inside a water tank was executed like the lowest common criminal.

THE ARCHERS LAY SIEGE TO EPHRON

During his military campaigns Judas Maccabeus frequently found himself obliged to lay siege to enemy cities. One day his army reached the walls of Ephron, a fortified city full of enemies from various parts; it was protected by ramparts and high towers from which machines of war would hurl enormous rocks down upon the attackers. Judas deployed his best archers in the front line; then, while they kept up a rain of arrows over the enemy battlements, he began to pray. Jehovah heard him, suggested the tactics he should follow for the assault, and, to the utter astonishment of the defenders, the Jews penetrated the outer walls, massacring those inside and looting everything within sight.

The death of Razis

The courage which the Israelites demonstrated as they were being pursued by the ruthless Nicanor sometimes reached sublime levels, as in the case of Razis, who was known as the Father of the Jews. Besieged in his own fortified house by a troop of enemy troops who were already setting fire to the vestibule, Razis felt that death was inevitable, so he threw himself on his sword rather than await the ignoble treatment which he knew would otherwise be his fate. But, since his wound was not fatal he managed to climb to the top of his tower and hurl himself at the attackers, who were so shocked that they stepped back suddenly. They then saw the man who had just fallen stand up again, dripping in blood, pull his own entrails from his body, and fall dead before them.

The death of Nicanor

The army of Judas Maccabeus found itself once again face to face with that of Nicanor which, on this occasion, was equipped with savage elephants and machines of war. In order to overcome the poor morale of his own men, who were reluctant to leave their camp to do battle, Judas told them of two dreams which Jehovah had sent him: in the first, the high priest Onias stretched out his hands in benediction over the Jewish nation, while in the second the prophet Jeremiah handed him a holy golden sword with which he was to destroy the enemy. The Jews immediately threw open the gates of the camp, rushed at Nicanor's troops and defeated them. Nicanor himself was unhorsed and captured. On the orders of Judas his head and one arm were cut off, his bloody remains were then hung up in full sight of the vanquished army and his tongue was cut out.

INDEX OF ILLUSTRATIONS FROM CODEX 1191 IN THE AUSTRIAN NATIONAL LIBRARY

P. 9

(Fol. 1r, whole page: 36 × 25 cm). Text page. Letter of St. Jerome to Paulinus. Initial F (rater) composed of double lines and interlaced knots on gold ground. Initial picture: St. Jerome in monastic habit seated at architectural desk. (Miniaturist I). Columns have borders with gold dots and grotesque ornamentation.

P. 11

(Fol. 466v, whole page: 36.3 × 25.7 cm). Page of text containing Psalms 67-68. Large initial S for Psalm 68 (Salvum me fac Deus...) with branching tracery, gold dots and grotesque ornamentation. Initial picture: the aged King David, naked with crown and halo, kneels in water and prays to God, whose head appears in a cloud. (Miniaturist II).

P. 12

(Fol. 26v, whole page: 36 × 25.5 cm). Text of Exodus Chapter 7 and beginning of Chapter 8. Columns set in borders with gold dots and grotesque ornamentation. Miniature at head of left-hand column (7.2 × 6.7 cm): Moses and Aaron addressing the Israelites. Miniature at foot of right-hand column (7.1 × 6.8 cm): changing of Aaron's staff into a serpent and water into blood. (Miniaturist IV).

P. 14, 15

(Fol. 460r, whole page: 36.1 × 25.7 cm). Page of text comprising Psalms 24-26. Two small initials with branching tracery. Large initial D for Psalm 26 (Dominus illuminatio mea...) with branching tracery, interlaced ornamentation and gold dots. Initial picture. King David enthroned, his right hand pointing to his eye and his left holding a scepter. (Miniaturist II).

P. 17, 18, 19

(Fol. 4r, whole page: 36 × 25 cm). Left-hand column giving the end of St. Jerome's Preface to Desiderius. Right-hand column composed of 4 miniatures of Genesis: creation of heaven and earth; creation of the creatures of the heaven, water and earth; creation of Adam; creation of Eve.

In each miniature God is depicted as the Trinity (a two-headed figure with dove). There are two miniatures at foot of page across both columns. Left-hand miniature: God leads Adam and Eve to the Tree of Knowledge. Right-hand miniature: the Fall of Man. (Miniaturist I).

Columns have borders with dots and grotesque ornamentation, angels, a knight and half-figures.

P. 20, 21

(Fol. 4r, miniature: 6.5 × 13.6 cm). Double miniature at foot of page across both columns. Left-hand half of picture: the expulsion from Paradise. Right-hand half of picture: Adam and Eve at their first work: Adam cultivates the soil, Eve spins. Between the two miniatures is the six-winged angel, in armor, with a flaming sword, standing before the gates of Paradise, above it a tree with a heron. (Miniaturist I).

P. 23, a

(Fol. 5r, miniature: 6.79 × 10.37 cm). Miniature at foot of page across both columns. Right-hand half of picture: Abel at prayer before the altar of burnt-offerings, Cain with averted face holding burning sheaves. Left-hand half of picture: Cain slays Abel. The figures are drawn larger than in the other miniatures by the same master. (Miniaturist I).

P. 23, b

(Fol. 6r, miniature: 6.5× 14 cm). Double miniature at foot of page across both columns. Left-hand miniature: God orders Noah to build the ark. Right-hand miniature: construction of the ark. (Miniaturist I).

P. 24, 25

(Fol. 6v, miniature: 5.9 × 10.38 cm). Double miniature at foot of page across both columns. Left-hand miniature: deluge, with Noah's head protruding from the ark and a dove flying towards him, an olive branch in its beak. Right-hand miniature: Noah's sacrifice, the animals walking onto dry land. (Miniaturist 1).

P. 26, a

(Fol. 7v, miniature: 8.1 × 14 cm). Miniature at foot of page across both columns: Tower of Babel. Left-hand half: the order to build the tower. Right-hand half: group of gesticulating Israelites in front of a building. (Miniaturist I).

P. 26, b

(Fol. 10v, miniature: 6 × 13.2 cm). Miniature at foot of page across both columns: destruction of Sodom. Left: Sodom in flames; center: Lot's wife turned to a pillar of salt; right: the aged Lot in flight with his daughters and sons-in-law. (Miniaturist I).

P. 28, 29

(Fol. 11r, miniature: 8.5 × 14.5 cm). Miniature at foot of page across both columns: the sacrifice of Isaac. Left-hand half: Abraham goes with his son Isaac and two servants to the place of sacrifice. Right-hand half: Abraham's hand is stayed from the sacrifice by an angel bringing a goat for slaughter instead. (Miniaturist I).

P. 30
(Fol. 17v, miniature: 7.2 × 6.5 cm). Miniature in right-hand column. Above: Joseph and his ten brethren grazing their father's goats. Below: Joseph complaining of his brethren to his father. (Miniaturist I).

P. 31
(Fol. 18v, miniature: 7.6 × 14.1 cm). Miniature at foot of page across both columns: Joseph's brethren bringing the bloodstained coat to the aged Jacob. (Miniaturist I).

P. 33
(Fol. 19r, miniature: 12.3 × 16.8 cm). Miniature at foot of page across both columns: Joseph sold by his brethren to the Ishmeelites for 20 silver coins. (Miniaturist I).

P. 34
(Fol. 19v, miniature: 5.9 × 4.5 cm). Miniature underneath left-hand column: Joseph and Potiphar's wife. (Miniaturist I).

P. 35
(Fol. 19v, miniature: 7.1 × 7.7 cm). Miniature at head of left-hand column: Joseph interpreting Pharaoh's dream. Left-hand background: Pharaoh and his consort asleep in a room. Foreground: representation of the dream, according to which (5) thin cows devour (4) fat cows. Right-hand background: Joseph, kneeling, interprets the dream for Pharaoh, enthroned. (Miniaturist I).

P. 36
(Fol. 20v, miniature: 7 × 6.1 cm). Miniature at head of right-hand column: Joseph and his brethren; twelve brethren kneel before Joseph, two bear bowls filled with coins. (Miniaturist II).

P. 37
(Fol. 21v, miniature: 7.1 × 7 cm). Miniature in centre of right-hand column: Joseph reveals himself to his brethren. (Miniaturist II).

P. 38
(Fol. 23r, miniature: 7.1 × 6.7 cm). Miniature in left-hand column: Jacob blesses the sons of Joseph, Ephraim and Manasseh, kneeling at his bedside; Joseph takes Jacob's hand. (Miniaturist IV).

P. 39
(Fol. 23v, miniature: 6.5 × 6.6 cm). Miniature at head of left-hand column: Jacob foretells his sons. (Miniaturist IV).

P. 40
(Fol. 24r, miniature: 7.5 × 6.8 cm). Miniature in center of right-hand column: entry of the sons of Israel into Egypt. (Miniaturist III).

P. 41
(Fol. 25c, miniature: 6.9 × 6.7 cm). Miniature in center of right-hand column: Moses kneeling before the burning bush; in foreground Moses once more chose staff in changing into a serpent. (Miniaturist IV).

P. 42
(Fol. 25v, miniature: 7× 7 cm). Miniature in center of right-hand column: Aaron wearing mitre welcomes and kisses Moses. (Miniaturist IV).

P. 43
(Fol. 27r, miniature: 7.1 × 6.7 cm). Miniature at foot of right-hand column: plague of frogs, gnats and flies; Aaron and Moses before Pharaoh enthroned. (Miniaturist IV).

P. 44
(Fol. 28v, miniature: 7.2 × 6.6 cm). Miniature at head of left-hand column: death of the first-born. Before the enthroned Pharaoh lie the corpses of the first-born men and beasts. On a hill Moses and Aaron pray to Jehovah. (Miniaturist IV).

P. 45
(Fol. 30r, miniature: 7.2 × 7.5 cm). Miniature at foot of left-hand column: crossing of the Red Sea. On the shore stand the Israelites, in the sea there are drowned Egyptians, animals and floating barrels. (Miniaturist IV).

P. 46
(Fol. 30 v, miniature: 7 × 6.7 cm). Miniature in center of left-hand column: fall of manna and miracle of the quails. Women gather up the manna falling from a cloud; Aaron and Moses praying to Jehovah. (Miniaturist IV).

P. 47
(Fol. 32r, miniature: 7.3 × 6.1 cm). Miniature at foot of left-hand column: giving of the tablets of the law on Mount Sinai. Moses praying to Jehovah. (Miniaturist IV).

P. 48
(Fol. 39v, miniature: 7.2 × 6.3 cm). Miniature in center of right-hand column: setting up of the ark of the covenant. Israelites use ropes to set up the tabernacle-like ark on a hill; before it Moses and Aaron in conversation. (Miniaturist IV).

P. 49
(Fol. 40r, miniature: 7.2 × 6.6 cm). Miniature at foot of left-hand column: Moses at prayer before the tabernacle. In the foreground Israelites bring animals for sacrifice. (Miniaturist IV).

P. 50
(Fol. 42r, miniature: 7 × 6.7 cm). Miniature at head of right-hand column: ordination of the priests. Moses ordains Aaron, a line of monks waits behind him. (Miniaturist IV).

P. 51
(Fol. 53r, miniature: 7.2 × 6.6 cm). Miniature at head of right-hand column: sacrifice of the princes of Israel. Moses sacrifices the animals brought by the princes. (Miniaturist IV).

P. 52
(Fol. 63r, miniature: 7.2 × 6.6 cm). Miniature at foot of right-hand column: Moses speaking to a group of Israelites, the sons of Ruben and Gad. Their herds graze in the foreground. (Miniaturist IV).

P. 53
(Fol. 65r, miniature: 7.2 × 6.7 cm). Miniature at foot of right-hand column: Moses standing on a hill addresses the listening Israelites. (Miniaturist IV).

P. 54
(Fol. 78r, miniature: 7.3 × 6.7 cm). Miniature in center of right-hand column: Jehovah calls Joshua. In the foreground the body of Moses on a couch. (Miniaturist IV).

P. 55
(Fol. 87v, miniature: 7.1 × 9.6 cm). Miniature at head of left-hand column: Joshua's death and the battle with the Canaanites. In the foreground rages the struggle between the Israelites and the Canaanites. In the background the body of Joshua lies on a hill. Judah and Simeon coming out of the city gate on the right. (Miniaturist IV).

P. 56
(Fol. 88v, miniature: 7.1 × 9.2 cm). Miniature in center of right-hand column: murder of Sisera. Jael drives a nail into the head of the Canaanite leader, Sisera. Left Barak and his horsemen clash with mounted Canaanites. (Miniaturist IV).

P. 58
(Fol. 90v, miniature: 7.1 × 9.8 cm). Miniature in center of right-hand column: Gideon and the Israelites cross the Jordan. (Miniaturist IV).

P. 59
(Fol. 94v, miniature: 7 × 6.7 cm). Miniature in center of left-hand column: in the foreground Delilah cutting off Samson's hair in a room. In the background Samson bearing the gates of Gaza. (Miniaturist IV).

P. 60
(Fol. 97v, miniature: 7× 6.6 cm). Miniature at foot of left-hand column: in the background Elimelech and his wife Naomi leaving their house, before them their sons Mahlon and Chilion. In the foreground the betrothal of the sons of Elimelech to the Moabite maidens Orpah and Ruth. (Miniaturist IV).

P. 61
(Fol. 99v, miniature: 7.2 × 6.7 cm). Miniature at head of right-hand column: in the foreground Elkanah between his wives Hannah and Peninnah and his eight sons. In the background Hannah goes to a high place and prays for a son in a temple. (Miniaturist IV).

P. 62
(Fol. 102r, miniature: 7.2 × 8.7 cm). Miniature at head of right-hand column: victory of the Israelites over the Philistines at Bethcar. On a hill Samuel holding a stone, which he puts between Maspath and Sen. (Miniaturist IV).

P. 63
(Fol. 107r, miniature: 7.2 × 7.5 cm). Miniature at head of right-hand column: David and Goliath. In the background on a hill the camp of the Israelites, from which David comes to do battle with Goliath. In the foreground David hurls the stone at the forehead of Goliath, who collapses streaming with blood. (Miniaturist IV).

P. 64
(Fol. 112v, miniature: 7.2 × 8.9 cm). Miniature at foot of right-hand column: death of Saul, Jonathan in a cavalry engagement with the Philistines. (Miniaturist IV).

P. 65
(Fol. 113r, miniature: 6.8 × 7 cm). Miniature in center of right-hand column: David orders the death of the Amalekite who brings back Saul's crown and bracelet. (Miniaturist IV).

P. 66
(Fol. 116r, miniature: 7.3 × 7.9 cm). Miniature at foot of left-hand column: David's victory over the Moabites. David on a white horse seizes the wagons of the conquered Moabites. (Miniaturist IV).

P. 67
(Fol. 120v, miniature: 6.8 × 8 cm). Miniature in center of left-hand column: the death of Absolom. Joab at the head of a group of horsemen strikes Absolom as he hangs from the tree. (Miniaturist IV).

P. 67
(Fol. 120v, miniature: 6.8 × 8 cm). Miniature in center of left-hand column: the death of Absalon. Joab at the head of a group of horsemen strikes Absalon as he hangs from the tree. (Miniaturist IV).

P. 68
(Fol. 134v, miniature: 7.2 × 9.1 cm). Miniature at head of left-hand column: Ahab's victory over the Syrians. Israelites pursue fleeing Syrians. (Miniaturist IV).

P. 69
(Fol. 136r, miniature: 7.3 × 7.9 cm). Miniature at head of right-hand column: right, the sick king Ahaziah orders messengers to consult Baalzebub, the god of Ekron, about his recovery. Left, Elijah dressed in animal skins, speaking with the king's emissary, on whom fire is streaming down.

P. 70
(Fol. 145v, miniature: 7.3 × 6.6 cm). Miniature at foot of left-hand column: in the background king Hezekiah lies in his bed praying for recovery. In the foreground Isaiah prophesies the king's return to health. (Miniaturist IV).

P. 71
(Fol. 159r, miniature: 7.5 × 6.8 cm). Miniature at foot of left-hand column: in the foreground Solmon asleep in his room, with Jehovah appearing to him in a dream. Above this, Solomon enthroned between two groups of Israelites. (Miniaturist IV).

P. 72
(Fol. 163v, miniature: 7.1 × 9.1 cm). Miniature at foot of left-hand column: mounted Israelites led by King Asa put the Ethiopians to flight. (Miniaturist IV).

P. 73
(Fol. 176v, miniature: 7.7 × 6.8 cm). Miniature at center of left-hand column: Nehemiah preaching to a crowd of men and women. (Miniaturist IV).

P. 74
(Fol. 182v, miniature: 7.3 × 6.9 cm). Miniature in lower half of right-hand column: King Josiah making a lassover burnt-offering. Left a group of Israelites approaching with sacrificial animals. (Miniaturist IV).

P. 75
(Fol. 188r, miniature: 7.2 × 6.6 cm). Miniature in center of right-hand column: Ezra teaching and audience from a book. Below this, seven Israelites sitting at a table with loaves on it. (Miniaturist IV).

P. 76
(Fol. 197r, miniature: 7.1 × 6.7 cm). Miniature in center of right-hand column: in background Tobias, giving alms to his relatives, with his wife Hannah. In foreground a man digging a grave for three bodies wrapped in shrouds—man murdered by Sennacherib being buried on Tobias's orders. (Miniaturist IV).

P. 77
(Fol. 201r, miniature: 6.9 × 7.3 cm). Miniature in center of left-hand column: victory of the Assyrians led by Nebuchadnezzar over the Medes led by King Arphaxad. (Miniaturist IV).

P. 78
(Fol. 204v, miniature: 7.4 × 7.2 cm). Miniature in lower half of right-hand column: the beheading of Holopherna. Right, the headless body of Holopherna in a tent mourned by Assyrians. Left Judits and her maid pass through the city gates, and from the city wall Judith raises up the head of Holopherna with her left hand, holding a sword in her right. In the background terrified Assyrians, in flight. (Miniaturist IV).

P. 79
(Fol. 206r, miniature: 7.2 × 6.8 cm). Miniature in lower half of left-hand column: the feast of King Xerxes. The guests sit at three tables in a garden. In the foreground Queen Vashti to whom a messenger is bringing a letter from the king. (Miniaturist IV).

P. 80
(Fol. 211r, miniature: 7.4 × 6.8 cm). Miniature in lower half of left-hand column: Job speaking with upraised hands to his seven sons and three daughters. (Miniaturist IV).

P. 81
(Fol. 22v, miniature: 6.8 × 6.1 cm). Miniature in center of left-hand column: King Solomon with crown and scepter seated on his throne, before him an audience. (Miniaturist IV).

P. 82
(Fol. 232v, miniature: 7 × 7 cm). Miniature in center of right-hand column: on a hill King Solomon with sword and balance sitting on a bench between four judges. Below, two groups of Israelites looking up at Solomon. (Miniaturist IV).

P. 83
(Fol. 253r, miniature: 7.1 × 6.7 cm). Miniature at foot of left-hand column: Isiah, with Jehovah appearing to him in a cloud. (Miniaturist IV).

P. 84
(Fol. 271v, miniature: 7.2 × 6.8 cm). Miniature at foot of left-hand column: Jeremiah, with Jehovah appearing to him in a cloud. (Miniaturist IV).

P. 85.
(Fol. 293v, miniature: 7.1 × 7 cm). Miniature in center of right-hand column: Baruch with a book in his hands in front of a group of Israelites. (Miniaturist IV).

P. 86, 87
(Fol. 296v, miniature: 7 × 6.8 cm). Miniature at head of left-hand column: the vision of Ezekiel. Above the river Shobar four animals: below left, a doglike animal with radiate head, right, a bear; above two winged lions, of which the left-hand one has tiny lion-heads in place of ears. (Miniaturist IV)

P. 88
(Fol. 315v, miniature: 7.2 × 6.9 cm). Miniature in center of right-hand column: King Nebuchadnezzar with crown and scepter enthroned on a hill, to whom the four royal youths, Daniel, Anasias, Misael and Azarias bring sacks from Jerusalem. Below, the four youths before their custodian, Malasar. (Miniaturist IV).

P. 89
(Fol. 317r, miniature: 7.2 × 6.8 cm). Miniature in lower half of right-hand column: the three youths in the fiery furnace. Left, King Nebuchadnezzar enthroned, next to him a fiddler. Center, a group at prayer round a golden idol. Right, the three youths Shadrach, Meshach and Abednego in the fiery furnace, guarded by an angel. On a salver in front of the fiery furnace lie the heads of the three men who had thrown the youths into the furnace and met their deaths thereby. (Miniaturist IV).

P. 90, 91
(Fol. 322v, miniature: 7.2 × 7.9 cm). Miniature in center of right-hand column: the story of Susanna. In the right foreground Susanna at the well being importuned by two elders. On a flight of steps Susanna between the two elders, who are giving false witness to the entrhoned Daniel. In left foreground: the stoning of the elders. (Miniaturist IV).

P. 92
(Fol. 324r, miniature: 7.3 × 6.7 cm). Miniature at foot of left-hand column: left on a hill, Hosea with Uzziah, Jotham, Ahaz, Hezekiah and Jeroboam, the five kings of his own making. Below, Hosea with his wife Gomer and his little son Jezreel. (Miniaturist IV).

P. 93
(Fol. 326v, miniature: 7.2 × 6.9 cm). Miniature in center of right-hand column: on a hill Joel foretells the devastation of Judea by a plague of locusts. Below, the felling of trees destroyed by the locusts. (Miniaturist IV).

P. 94
(Fol. 328r, miniature: 7.3 × 6.7 cm). Miniature at head of left-hand column: on a hill Amos foretells to Kings Uzziah and Jeroboam and a group of Israelites the doom of Damascus, Gaza, Tyre and Edom. (Miniaturist IV).

P. 95
(Fol. 330r, miniature: 7 × 6.7 cm). Miniature in lower half of left-hand column: on a hill Abdias, to whom Jehovah appears. Below, a group of soldiers. (Miniaturist IV).

P. 96
(Fol. 330v, miniature: 7.2 × 6.7 cm). Miniature in upper half of left-hand column: Jonah. In the background Jonah falls from his ship into the sea. In the foreground Jonah is spewed up on the beach by the fish. On land a king in penitential garb is leaving the gates of a city. (Miniaturist IV).

P. 97
(Fol. 331r,, miniature: 7.2 × 6.7 cm). Miniature in center of right-hand column: Micah, naked, foretells the punishment of Jerusalem and Samaria to Kings Jotham, Ahaz and Hezekiah. (Miniaturist IV).

P. 98, 99
(Fol. 332v, miniature: 7.1 × 6.9 cm). Miniature at foot of right-hand column: Nahum, to whom Jehovah is appearing in a cloud. (Miniaturist IV).

P. 100
(Fol. 333v, miniature: 7.3 ×ˆ6.3 cm). Miniature in lower half of left-hand column: on a hill Habakkuk, to whom Jehovah is appearing in a cloud. In right foreground a group of mounted soldiers. (Miniaturist IV).

P. 101
(Fol. 334v, miniature: 7.3 × 6.7 cm). Miniature at head of left-hand column: on a hill Zephaniah, to whom Jehovah is appearing in a cloud. In the foreground men, fishes, birds, sheep and cattle which are to be exterminated by Zephaniah at Jehovah's command. (Miniaturist IV).

P. 102
(Fol. 335r, miniature: 7.3 × 6.9 cm). Miniature in lower half of right-hand column: on a hill Haggai appearing before Zerubbabel, the prince of Judah, and Joshua, the High Priest, to exhort them to build the Temple. Below in foreground: work on the Temple goes ahead. (Miniaturist IV).

P. 103
(Fol. 336r, miniature: 7.1 × 6.8 cm). Miniature in center of left-hand column: the visions of Zechariah. On a hill two pairs of angels holding silver flasks. In the background a tabernacle and, suspended in the air, the lamp-stand with seven lamps. In the foreground between golden mountains two chariots. One chariot has a red horse before it and another inside it. The other chariot has white horses similarly placed. (Miniaturist IV).

P. 104
(Fol. 342r, miniature: 6.8 × 9.2 cm). Miniature in center of left-hand column: Judas Maccabaeus at the head of his horsemen pursues the fleeing Syrians. (Miniaturist IV).

P. 105
(Fol. 345v, miniature: 7.2 × 7.9 cm). Miniature in the lower half of right-hand column: Nicanor (?) at the head of his cavalry before a building. The soldiers looking down from it have orders to seize Judas. In front of the building an ambassador from Nicanor kneels before Judas Maccabaeus. (Miniaturist IV).

P. 106
(Fol. 347r, miniature: 7.2 × 7.5 cm). Miniature at head of left-hand column: in the foreground the battle of the Bacchides with the Israelites. On a hill the burial of Judas Maccabaeus by his followers. (Miniaturist IV).

P. 107
(Fol. 348r, miniature: 9.1 × 6.8 cm). Miniature at foot of right-hand column: on a hill Jonathas Maccabaeus being handed a letter by messengers from Demetrius. In the foreground victory of the troops of Alexander Epiphanes over those of Demetrius. (Miniaturist IV).

P. 108
(Fol. 349v, miniature: 7.2 × 9.2 cm). Miniature in upper half of right-hand column: Israelites rescue King Demetrius Nicator of Syria from an uprising in Antioch. Left, the king in his palace, protected by archers. Right in background Antioch in flames. (Miniaturist IV).

P. 109
(Fol. 350r, miniature: 7.3 × 7.8 cm). Miniature in center of left-hand column: in a mountain landscape left Jonathas Maccabaeus as High Priest riding with Mathathias and Judas, before them fleeing pagans. (Miniaturist IV).

P. 110
(Fol. 350v, miniature: 7.2 × 7.7 cm). Miniature in upper half of left-hand column: victory of Jonathas Maccabaeus over the army of Demetrius Nicator. On a hill Jonathas, enthroned, listens to the reports of his scouts. (Miniaturist IV).

P. 112
(Fol. 352v, miniature: 7.2 × 7.9 cm). Miniature at foot of right-hand column: on a hill Simon Maccabaeus and his sons Judas and John, who are to lead the people. In foreground separated by a stream, left the Israelite army, right the fleeing soldiers of Cendebaeus, Antiochus' general. (Miniaturist IV).

P. 113
(Fol. 353r, miniature: 8.2 × 6.8 cm). Miniature at head of right-hand column: on a hill messengers from a group of Jews in Egypt bring letters from Judaea. In lower foreground Feast of Tabernacles with burnt-offering of animals on an altar. (Miniaturist IV).

P. 114
(Fol. 357v, miniature: 7.2 × 8.1 cm). Miniature in upper half of left-hand column: victory of Israelites under Judas Maccabaeus over the soldiers of Nicanor. (Miniaturist IV).

P. 115
(Fol. 358v, miniature: 7.1 × 8.3 cm). Miniature in center of right-hand column: Judas Maccabaeus in full armor, surrounded by five angels in armor with golden swords and shields, before the dead of the army of Timotheus. (Miniaturist IV).

P. 116
(Fol. 359v, miniature: 7.3 × 7.4 cm). Miniature at foot of right-hand column: the city of Ephron besieged by archers, at whom soldiers are hurling stones from the city walls. In right foreground Judas Maccabaeus, armored and mounted, with his entourage. (Miniaturist IV).

P. 117, 118
(Fol. 361v, double miniature: 14.9 × 7 cm). Two miniatures one above the other, occupying the lower half of the right-hand column. Upper miniature (7.2 × 6 cm): death of Razis. In the background Razis hurls himself down from a building before the soldiers of Nicanor can break open the doors. In the foreground the dying Razis, who tears out his own entrails. Lower miniature (7.7 × 7 cm): death of Nicanor. The victorious Jews ride over the corpse of Nicanor. (Miniaturist IV).

(Notes by
Eva Irblich)